Empire of Ancient Rome

MICHAEL BURGAN

☑®

Facts On File, Inc.

Great Empires of the Past: EMPIRE OF ANCIENT ROME

Copyright © 2005 Michael Burgan

HISTORY CONSULTANT: Clifford Ando, Ph.D., Associate Professor of Classics, University of Southern California

Facts On File, Inc.
132 West 31st Street
New York NY 10001

Library of Congress Cataloging-in-Publication Data
Burgan, Michael.
Empire of Ancient Rome / Michael Burgan.
p. cm. – (Great empires of the past)
Includes bibliographical references and index.
ISBN 0-8160-5559-9 (hc: alk. paper)
1. Rome–History–Juvenile literature. 2. Rome–Social life and
customs–Juvenile literature. I. Title. II. Series.
DG209.B87 2004
937'–dc22   2004003953

Facts On File books are available at special discounts when purchased in bulk quantities for businesses, associations, institutions, or sales promotions. Please call our Special Sales Department in New York at (212) 967-8800 or (800) 322-8755.

You can find Facts On File on the World Wide Web at http://www.factsonfile.com

Produced by the Shoreline Publishing Group LLC
Editorial Director: James Buckley Jr.
Series Editor: Beth Adelman
Designed by Thomas Carling, Carling Design, Inc.
Photo research by Jullie Chung, PhotoSearch Inc., New York
Index by Word Co.

Photo and art credits: Scala/Art Resource, NY: 1, 12, 67, 78, 96, 106, 115; SEF/Art Resource, NY: 3, 11, 107; Erich Lessing/Art Resource, NY: 4, 14, 53, 55, 109; Alinari/Art Resource, NY: 17, 39, 64, 74, 83, 94; Sally Webb/Lonely Planet Images: 27; Jon Davison/Lonely Planet Images: 30; Giraudon/Bridgeman Art Library: 33; The Stapleton Collection/ Bridgeman Art Library: 37; Facts On File: 45, 116; Cameraphoto Arte, Venice/Art Resource, NY: 46; Bridgeman Art Library: 50; Eddie Gerald/Lonely Planet Images: 58; Detail from The Metropolitan Museum of Art, Rogers Fund, 1903. (03.14.5): 62; Associated Press, U.S. Senate: 70; Giraudon/Art Resource, NY: 86, 112; Glenn Beanland/Lonely Planet Images: 93; Charlotte Hindle/Lonely Planet Images:110; John Griffin/The Image Works: 118

Printed in the United States of America

VB PKG 10 9 8 7 6 5 4 3 2 1

This book is printed on acid-free paper.

CONTENTS

Introduction

ANCIENT ROME—THE NAME SUGGESTS MILITARY AND economic power, detailed laws, political skill and intrigue, masterful literature, and massive buildings that have stood for more than 2,000 years. Rome represents the greatness an empire can achieve. It also reminds us that even the most powerful empires decline and crumble over time. At least one historian has claimed that studying the rise and fall of Rome presents the two most complex topics any historian can tackle. The people, places, and ideas of the Roman Empire still fascinate us.

The Romans left behind many books that explain their empire and the lives of its citizens. (Unfortunately, even more writings did not survive to modern times.) These writers, like authors and historians today, describe the world as they saw it, bringing their personal feelings and ideas into their work. Current historians of Rome try to balance these sometimes conflicting views to find the truth about the empire. The modern historians also consider the remains found by archaeologists. Artifacts—common items from everyday life—provide concrete evidence about this ancient world.

Why would an empire that fell more than 1,500 years ago interest us today? Its language, Latin, is often said to be "dead" because no modern nation speaks it. The gods and myths that shaped its religions seem like fairy tales.

Rome, however, laid the foundation for many of the institutions and ideas common in the modern Western world. Geographically, "the West" generally refers to the countries of Europe and the lands their citizens settled. Culturally, almost the entire world has felt the influence of the West, through trade or direct political control. Western influence means some degree of Roman influence—especially its ideas about politics, society, and culture. The Roman Empire also strengthened the Christian religion, which today touches people on every continent.

The Roman Empire also remains important because of the lessons it can teach today's leaders and philosophers. Livy (59 B.C.E.–17 C.E.), a Roman historian, wrote (as quoted by Jo-Ann Shelton in *As the Romans Did*) that after reading history, "you may choose for yourself and for your own community what to imitate." Roman history offers many examples of the finest human traits—ones anyone might want to copy. That history also illustrates actions and attitudes nations and peoples might want to avoid.

A Growing Village

Rome started out as a simple village spread out among seven hills in the central Italian peninsula, near the Tiber River. The river flows into the Tyrrhenian Sea, part of the much larger Mediterranean Sea. According to tradition, Rome was founded in 753 B.C.E., but people actually first settled in the region hundreds of years before then. Tribes in the region included the Latins, the Sabines, and the Etruscans, who were all influenced by their neighbors to the south and east, the Greeks.

Rome began as a monarchy, ruled by legendary kings who held military and political powers that were known collectively as *imperium*. (This word is the root of the English words *imperial, empire,* and *emperor.*) The king received advice from a group of prominent Roman citizens, known as patricians. These people, mostly wealthy landowners, were the descendants of a group of families that had belonged to the aristocracy at the beginning of the sixth century B.C.E. They formed what was later called the Senate. Around 500 B.C.E., the patricians rebelled and forced the king from power. Under the Senate's rule, Rome's form of government was called a republic. The period when the Senate dominated Rome is also called the Republic.

Over time, the Senate shared some of its power with the plebs (also called plebeians), the larger class of Romans who were not patricians. The plebs formed their own government body, including an assembly, and they elected leaders called tribunes. The Senate still dominated the government, but the tribunes could veto certain Senate decrees.

Under both the monarchy and the Republic, Rome expanded its borders. It defeated the Etruscans and other neighboring tribes, who then agreed to fight with Rome against any invading enemy. Rome emerged as the most powerful city in the area known as Latium. Over the next few centuries, the Roman Empire continued to grow.

WHAT ARE CONNECTIONS?

Throughout this book, and all the books in the Great Empires of the Past series, you will find Connections boxes. They point out ideas, inventions, art, food, customs, and more from this empire that are still part of our world today. Nations and cultures in remote history can seem far removed from our world, but these connections demonstrate how our everyday lives have been shaped by the peoples of the past.

Rome and the World Outside

As the Roman Republic first took shape, empires had already formed in the regions around the Mediterranean Sea. Egypt reached its peak around 1400 B.C.E., spreading its influence into parts of eastern Asia. The region we call the Middle East had seen the rise and fall of several powerful peoples, including the Babylonians, the Hittites, and the Assyrians. Their lands included parts of modern-day Turkey and Iraq. In Persia—today's Iran—an empire first developed around 1750 B.C.E. and lasted for more than 1,000 years.

Around 700 B.C.E., various independent Greek cities, called city-states, began to emerge as powerful centers of trade along the Mediterranean and the Black Sea. Athens, one of these city-states, became a center of literature and philosophy, producing such great thinkers as Plato (c. 427–347 B.C.E.) and Aristotle (384–322 B.C.E.). Athens also developed a democratic political system, with decisions made collectively by all the free male citizens. (Women and slaves did not play a role in the political process in Greece or Rome.)

Athens reached its peak as the premier Greek city in the mid-fifth century B.C.E. In the next century, Macedonia, just north of Athens, developed into the most powerful state in the region. It developed an effective army, and under King Philip II (382–336 B.C.E.), the Macedonians took control of their Greek neighbors. In 334 B.C.E., Philip's son Alexander (356–323 B.C.E.) began a war of conquest that took him through Egypt, Persia, and Central Asia into India. When he was done, Alexander was known as "the Great," and he ruled the largest empire the world had so far seen. Alexander's empire did not last long, but Greek culture continued to influence the eastern Mediterranean region and parts of Asia.

Rome, which had first experienced Greek culture (also known as

CONNECTIONS >>>>>>>>>>>>

Republics and Democracies

The English word *republic* comes from the Latin *res publica*, meaning "public things," or the people's common concerns. Today *republic* is used to define a type of government in which voters elect representatives who serve their interests in a central assembly of lawmakers. The republican system works at all levels of government—local, state, and national. The U.S. political system is also called a democracy, or democratic republic. In the world of the ancient Greeks and Romans, however, a democracy meant all voters met face-to-face and decided political issues for themselves, not through elected representatives. The word *democracy* comes from the Greek *demos*, which means "people." The two major U.S. political parties, the Republicans and Democrats, take their names from *republic* and *democracy*.

Hellenism) largely through the Etruscans, made more direct contact with the Greeks at the start of the third century B.C.E. By then Rome had already spread its influence northward in the Italian peninsula and was moving southward as well. The Greeks controlled several cities in the southern half of the Italian peninsula, and some of them struck alliances with Rome rather than risk being attacked by its increasingly powerful army. With its new Greek allies and later expansion into Greece itself, Rome became more Hellenized. The Roman culture that developed under the empire blended Hellenistic ideas with the culture of other peoples and native Roman ideas. This so-called Greco-Roman culture became the foundation for Western culture, and it influenced Arab culture as well.

Wars of Expansion

After its conquest of most of the Italian peninsula—including the islands of Sicily and Sardinia—Rome focused its military might on countries beyond its borders. Starting around 230 B.C.E., it fought Illyria, a kingdom along the northern Adriatic Sea. The Republic wanted to end Illyrian pirate raids on Roman ships. With its successes, Rome won influence in several Greek cities in Illyria. Rome then slowly extended its control further into the Balkans, the region of Europe bordered by the Adriatic, Black, and Mediterranean Seas.

Roman troops also fought the Republic's neighbors to the north, the Gauls. This tribe was related to the Celtic people who first settled Ireland and England. The Gauls lived in what is now France and Belgium, as well as the northern edge of modern Italy. The Romans battled the Gauls for centuries, and after 200 B.C.E. Roman troops advanced farther into their lands.

For more than 50 years, Rome's most threatening foe was Carthage. The Carthaginians were descendants of the Phoenicians. Starting around 1200 B.C.E., the Phoenicians built a series of city-states based on their sea trade in the Mediterranean. Carthage was a Phoenician city that built its own empire along the coast of North Africa and parts of the Iberian Peninsula—modern-day Spain and Portugal. As Rome became a major power in the western Mediterranean, it fought several wars with Carthage. These wars are now known as the Punic Wars, after the Roman name for the Carthaginians: Poenus. After defeating Carthage in 202 B.C.E., Rome was the master of the region, although it did not take direct control of all Carthaginian lands until a little more than 50 years later.

Rome had several advantages as it expanded across Italy and then beyond its borders. The city developed around farmlands that provided plenty of food for a growing population. Rome also had access to a major

ALEXANDER THE GREAT

Alexander the Great was just 21 years old when he took over the kingdom of Macedonia. Almost immediately, he began a grand military campaign that lasted until his death. Romans and other ancient people considered him the greatest general ever—the standard used to judge other military leaders who followed him. In his biography of Julius Caesar (100–44 B.C.E.), the historian Plutarch (c. 46–c. 120) wrote that the great Roman general wept after reading about Alexander's life. "'Do you think,' said [Caesar], 'I have not just cause to weep, when I consider that Alexander at my age had conquered so many nations, and I have all this time done nothing that is memorable.'"

river and the sea, helping its trade. It had a central location on the Italian peninsula and could easily send troops in any direction. The Romans believed their gods had chosen them to rule a growing empire. Rome's leaders granted political rights to most defeated foes, making them more willing to peacefully accept Roman rule. That peace, in turn, helped the empire's trade expand, and wealth from the outer areas flowed back to Rome. Rome was able to draw on the best ideas of the people around it—especially the Greeks—and add its own strengths of discipline and organization.

Trouble at Home

As the empire grew, Rome itself could not avoid political and social problems. The wealthy increased their land holdings, while the poor struggled to pay their bills. In 133 B.C.E., Tiberius Gracchus, a political leader of the plebs, emerged to challenge the interests of the wealthy and seek land for the poor. His brother Gaius took over this effort after Tiberius was killed. The two believed Rome had to address the needs of the poor to prevent rebellion. The wealthy citizens of Rome, however, were not eager to give up their land or their power. Tiberius also sidestepped some Roman laws to try to achieve his goal, which further angered the conservatives.

Military threats followed these political troubles, as Rome lost battles in Macedonia and Germanic tribes were advancing on Roman lands to the north and west. The Roman Republic fought a series of wars into the first century B.C.E., with some taking place within the Italian peninsula against tribes that were supposed to be its allies. Roman leaders broke into factions, and generals competed for the best assignments. In 88 B.C.E. forces led by rival generals Marius and Sulla clashed within the city of Rome. Sulla won the civil war and emerged as the dictator. (In Rome, *dictator* was a formal position given to generals for a limited time. Now, the word is used in a general sense to describe a leader who uses military power to deny individual liberties and preserve his rule.)

For the next 50 years, several Roman generals struggled to win

CONNECTIONS >>>>>>>>>>>>>

Plebs and Patricians

The names of the first two political associations in Rome, the plebs and the patricians, still appear in English today. A patrician is someone who comes from a wealthy background. The word also describes something connected with wealth and power. Plebeian is another name for a common person or something that is considered crude. Plebe, another form of the word, is also the term used for first-year students at some naval or military academies.

Hail Caesar!

As emperor, Octavian was sometimes called Caesar, in honor of his uncle, Julius Caesar. Future emperors also used the name in their title. Today, *caesar* can refer to anyone who rules with complete power. The name also led to the Russian word *czar* and the German word *kaiser*—titles for former royal rulers in Russia and Germany.

control of the government, even as they continued to fight foreign enemies and gain new territory. Finally, in February 44 B.C.E., Julius Caesar was named dictator for life. His reign, however, ended before it really began. His political enemies in the Senate murdered him the next month. Rome then fell into another chaotic period of civil war until Octavian (63 B.C.E.–14 C.E.), Julius Caesar's nephew, emerged as the new leader—and Rome's first emperor.

The True Roman Empire

Octavian took the name Augustus, which means "honored" or "revered." The long years of turmoil convinced the Senate that Rome needed a single powerful ruler to restore order. Augustus did not seize power—he made sure the Senate granted him control, so no one could accuse him of being a tyrant. Still, Augustus ruled as an emperor, taking full control of the government, even though the Senate technically kept some powers for itself.

The vast areas Rome controlled under the Republic were now part of a true empire. These lands included all of Gaul and Iberia, large parts of the Balkans, and the sections of the Middle East bordering the Mediterranean. Augustus's main job was to preserve the peace within the Italian peninsula and keep foreign lands under Roman control. His reign brought what was called the Pax Romana, or "Roman Peace."

After Augustus, the next four emperors were all related to him in some way, establishing the first Roman dynasty (a government ruled by one family for several generations). Emperors tried to make sure they had a son or other relation who could take power after them, although the Senate and especially the army played a role in deciding who became emperor. The transition from one emperor to another could be bloody. Rome went through another civil war around 69, a year when four different men briefly served as emperor.

Even with the political uncertainties, Rome kept growing, especially when popular and effective emperors ruled. Two of the best were Trajan (53–117) and Hadrian (76–138). Trajan extended the empire in the east, into the lands between the Caspian and Black Seas. Hadrian gave back some of these gains, but he strengthened Roman control in England, the farthest extent of the empire in Western Europe.

Several dynasties ruled between 69 and 192, including the Flavian and Antonine. The next major dynasty began in 193, with Septimius Severus (146–211). This Severan Dynasty lasted until 235. Septimius gave the military a larger role in Roman society, and when his dynasty ended, ambitious generals tried to win the support of Roman troops, who often chose the next emperor.

A Slow Decline

Rome's troubles increased as foreign forces grew more powerful. In the north and west of Europe, Germanic tribes threatened imperial lands. In Asia Minor, the Sassanians, a renewed Persian kingdom, fought Roman troops. The emperors had to spend more money fighting distant wars, which harmed the economy of the empire. At the same time, the emperors had to give up some political rule in the provinces—lands conquered and controlled by Rome—to local officials.

In 286, the emperor Diocletian (245–316) decided to share power with a co-emperor; each took responsibility for one part of the empire. This division remained in place for more than 200 years. One of the exceptions came under Constantine the Great (285–337), who ruled over a united empire from 324 to 337. Constantine is best remembered for being the first emperor to convert to Christianity, a religion that developed in Roman lands after the death of Jesus Christ around 29. Constantine also moved the empire's capital to Byzantium, a small city in what is now Turkey. The city's name was later changed to Constantinople and is today called Istanbul.

Hadrian's Wall
In northern England, Hadrian built a wall to prevent hostile tribes from attacking areas under Roman control. The wall stretched for about 80 miles, from Maia (modern-day Bowness) on the west coast to Segedunum (Wallsend) on the east coast. The stone wall was between 15 to 20 feet high with small forts and watchtowers all along it. Parts of the wall still stand.

11

Heart of the Catholic Church

Rome eventually became the seat of Western Christianity. This is St. Peter's Basilica in Vatican City, an independent state in the heart of Rome run by the Roman Catholic Church. The official language here is Latin.

The empire split again after Constantine. Over the next few decades, the western half faced growing attacks from so-called barbarian invaders. Going into the fifth century, German chieftains took control of larger parts of the empire. The Romans by this time relied on friendly Germanic tribes for military aid, and some of the best German soldiers were important generals for Rome. In 476, German soldiers named one of their commanders the emperor in the west, marking the end of the western half of the Roman Empire. The eastern Roman Empire, however, survived, with Constantinople as its capital. It became the Byzantine Empire, which lasted for almost another 1,000 years.

Still, the idea of Rome as the center of a great empire was not completely dead. The city became the home of the leader of the Christian church in Western Europe–the pope. The church used Latin, the language of Rome, in its services and drew on Roman law and literature. This Christian church is today called the Roman Catholic Church. It served as a link between ancient Rome and the political and social structures that followed it in Western Europe.

Rome's rise and fall took place over 1,000 years. During that time, the Romans ruled a larger empire than any people before them. The Roman Empire also lasted longer than any other government ever created in the West. Its society, according to Finley Hooper in *Roman Realities*, thrived because of "tradition, education, and family pride." Yet the empire collapsed more because of breakdowns in that society, not dangers from outside. The appeal of the old ways lost out to a lust for power and wealth, along with economic and political forces the emperors could not or would not control. Roman history is filled with abusive leaders and the use of force to expand the empire's borders. Most people of the era lived in poverty and had limited legal rights. Still, the great things that Rome accomplished remain part of the foundation of the modern Western world.

PART I

HISTORY

The Birth and Growth of Rome

The Empire at Its Peak

The Decline and Fall of Rome

CHAPTER 1

The Birth and Growth of Rome

HUMAN LIFE IN WHAT IS NOW ITALY DATES BACK TO AT LEAST 700,000 B.C.E. The Romans did not have evidence of these early hunters and gatherers, so they relied on legends to mark the start of their history. During the rule of Augustus Caesar, the date of April 21, 753 B.C.E., was accepted for the founding of Rome. The founder, Romulus, was said to have been a descendent of Aeneas, a Greek hero who fled his homeland of Troy and settled in Latium. The name of this region in central Italy is the root of the English word *Latin*, the language the Romans spoke. *Latin* also refers to one of the tribes of Latium.

The story of Romulus is part of modern legends as well. Students still learn that he and his brother Remus were the sons of Mars, the Roman god of war, and Rhea Silvia, who was related to Aeneas. The two brothers were abandoned, left to die in a basket sent down a river. Instead, a female wolf found them and raised them. As adults the two brothers decided to found a city near the spot where they were rescued as babies. Romulus then killed Remus when they argued over who would rule their new city, which became Rome.

The truth of Rome's founding lacks the drama and bloodshed of Romulus's tale. The city began as a series of villages that dotted seven hills near the Tiber River. The hills gave the residents a good view of the countryside and were easy to defend from enemy attack. The river gave the early Romans access to foreign trade.

The Latins dominated the seven hills of early Rome. Their neighbors in the central Italian peninsula included the Sabines, Samnites, Campani, and Volsci. The most important group, however, was the Etruscans, who dominated the central part of the Italian peninsula. The Etruscans' land,

OPPOSITE
The Face of Caesar
Julius Caesar remains one of the most controversial figures in Roman history. His skills as a military leader expanded the Roman Empire and brought great wealth and political stability. But he also became the first absolute ruler, overthrowing 500 years of democracy and changing Rome forever.

15

Etruria, was just north of Rome along the Italian peninsula's western coast. (Modern Italy's Tuscany region is named for them.) The Etruscans traded with the Greeks and Phoenicians, who shared their cultures. The Greeks were especially crucial in shaping Etruscan culture. By 750 B.C.E., the Greeks were starting small colonies in parts of the Italian peninsula, as well as trading with the Etruscans and other Italian peoples. The Greeks were part of a thriving system of trade carried out across the eastern Mediterranean Sea. The Etruscans offered them and other distant traders a variety of natural resources, including copper, tin, olive oil, and grains. As trade increased, the Etruscans built larger towns and cities, which united in leagues.

The Roman Kingdom

Although Rome was not founded in 753 B.C.E., important changes did take place there around that time. The small villages on the hills grew into a unified town, as trade and farming increased. The people of these villages were linked by shared religious beliefs, which included the worship of many gods and goddesses. Around 625 B.C.E. the Latins drained a marshy area to create Rome's first major forum, where people gathered to carry out politics and buy and sell goods. To some historians, this period marks the true founding of Rome as a distinct city.

As Rome developed it was ruled by kings. These kings, however, did not have absolute power. They worked with political bodies called assemblies, which were made up of the city's soldiers. The kings also sought advice from the Senate, a group of the wealthiest and most influential citizens. The first members of the Senate were known as *patres*, which means "fathers."

Under the kings Rome slowly expanded its borders into neighboring tribal areas. To fight its neighbors, Rome developed an army with both an infantry (foot soldiers) and cavalry (soldiers on horseback). Originally the army was organized around the three major tribes in the city, with each tribe expected to provide 1,000 troops. The tribes were further split into 10 groups, and each group provided 100 men. These 100 troops were called a century, and one soldier was a centurion. (The English words *cent* and *century* come from the Latin word *centum*, which means "100.") Together the 3,000 soldiers were called a legion.

Every Roman who owned property was expected to serve in the military. The wealthiest citizens, who could afford horses and other supplies, formed the cavalry. The Romans called these soldiers *equites*. The infantry was split into different classes, depending on how much land or other

THE ETRUSCANS

For many years, historians had trouble uncovering details about the Etruscans. Their language used letters similar to the ones in the Greek alphabet, but their words were totally different from the other ancient languages of the Mediterranean region. The Etruscan writings that have been discovered have not yet been translated, although experts have been able to understand enough words to get a rough idea of some of the concepts expressed in these writings. Most information about the Etruscans comes from the art and artifacts they left behind. Ancient Greek and Roman historians sometimes described the Etruscans, but these descriptions were written to serve the interests of the Greeks or Romans and not all of the information is correct.

wealth a person owned. The premier infantry was the hoplite. These soldiers carried round shields and spears and marched in a tight formation into battle. Their name came from the Greek word *hoplon*, which means a tool or weapon. The Greeks had first developed the hoplite's battle techniques, and the Romans borrowed them. Throughout their history the Romans quickly adapted weapons and tactics used by their neighbors and enemies, then usually improved their use on the battlefield.

Enduring Legend
The legend of Romulus and Remus founding Rome is still widely popular. This figure of the two young boys being cared for by a wolf is found on many public buildings all over Rome today.

First Wars and Conquest

Roman historians wrote that during the sixth century B.C.E., their kings began to rule as tyrants. Ancient sources say that in 509 B.C.E. the Roman people rebelled against the king and created the Republic. Two leaders, called consuls, were elected each year. They worked with the Senate and a body called the Centuriate Assembly.

By this time, Rome's lands covered about 300 square miles and included up to 40,000 people. According to the ancient sources, Rome fought a series of wars against the Etruscans as it went from the monarchy to a republican government. Next, the Romans battled a group of Latin cities called the Latin League. The Romans won a close victory in 499 B.C.E., and a few years later the two sides signed a peace treaty that formed an alliance.

Under the treaty, each side agreed to help the other if it was attacked or wanted military aide. In this new Latin League, Rome was the major power and it received half of all the land and wealth captured during wars. The other half was split between the other Latin cities. With every success on the battlefield, Rome was guaranteed to grow larger than its neighbors.

Rome's main foe during the fifth century B.C.E. was the Etruscan city Veii. Located about 10 miles north of Rome along the Tiber River, Veii was rich and powerful. Rome and Veii competed to control the salt beds along the river. Salt was an important resource in ancient times and it played a major role in foreign trade. Each city also wanted to dominate the trade routes along the Tiber. Starting around 481 B.C.E., the Romans and the Veians fought a series of wars. Rome finally triumphed in 396, after a long siege of Veii. With its victory Rome almost doubled its territory in the central part of the Italian peninsula, and won increasing respect among other Etruscan cities and the Greeks.

Rome's fortunes, however, suffered during the 390s B.C.E., as it faced an invasion from the north. The Gauls had been moving across the Alps into the northern part of the Italian peninsula for more than 100 years. With a fleet cavalry and soldiers who swung large, heavy swords, the Gauls captured land from the Etruscans. The Romans began to call this region Gallia Cisalpina, or Cisalpine Gaul, meaning "Gaul this side of the Alps."

As the Gauls continued to move south, the Romans tried to sign a peace treaty with them. This diplomatic effort failed, and the Romans then sent out an army of 10,000 to 15,000 men—the largest force they had ever assembled. Still, the Gauls defeated this huge force and began a siege of Rome. The Gauls finally left when they learned that their homeland was under attack—and after the Romans gave them 1,000 pounds of gold.

Expanding the Republic

Rome rebuilt quickly after the Gallic invasion and re-emerged as the main power in the central part of the Italian peninsula. Still, other cities challenged Rome, leading to another series of war. In 343 B.C.E., the Romans fought the Samnites, an association of tribes to the southeast. After a Roman victory two years later, the two sides became allies. They then joined together to fight the tribes in the Latin League, who were beginning to challenge Rome's authority. This so-called Latin War ended in 338 B.C.E. with another Roman victory.

After the war, the Latin League was dissolved and Rome was clearly the dominant force in the region. Rome took control of some of the territory held by the Latin cities. Other defeated peoples kept their independence, but they were expected to provide military aid when Rome asked for it.

Rome also expanded by founding colonies. Settlers agreed to give up their Roman citizenship in return for land. The new colonial towns were called Latin colonies, as they received the same rights held in the past by the members of the Latin League. Smaller settlements, known as Roman colonies, were usually military posts. Roman citizens who moved to these colonies kept their Roman citizenship. Rome's influence also grew by signing treaties with other tribes and winning more victories on the battlefield.

SIEGE WARFARE

Laying siege to an enemy city is an ancient military tactic. The Greeks did it before the Romans, but the Romans were particularly effective in capturing enemy cities using a siege. The basic idea of a siege is to surround a city and prevent the citizens from receiving supplies—food, water, and weapons. Then, when the enemy is weakened, the siege forces can attack. Before that point, however, the city under siege might decide to surrender. At Veii the Romans finally ended their siege after they used a tunnel to sneak soldiers underneath the city's defensive walls and into the city itself.

Rome's continuing growth led to two more wars with the Samnites. Around 327 B.C.E., the former allies supported opposing sides in a political struggle in the city of Naples. Their war ended more than 20 years later in a draw, and a third Samnite war began in 298 B.C.E. This time, the Samnites called on the Gauls and Etruscans for help, but in the end Rome and its allies won a major victory. In 290 B.C.E. the Samnites came under Roman control, and within the next two decades Rome had also defeated the Gauls and the Etruscans. The Roman Empire was now secure in the central part of the Italian peninsula.

With Roman influence spreading farther south, the Republic came into conflict with the Greek city of Tarentum (the modern city of Taranto). Rome made alliances with several smaller Greek cities in the southern part of the Italian peninsula, challenging Tarentum's dominance. In 280 B.C.E., a Greek force led by King Pyrrhus (c. 318–272 B.C.E.) invaded Roman lands. Pyrrhus won several victories but suffered heavy losses, and today the phrase "Pyrrhic victory" describes any victory that is eventually more damaging to the winner than the loser. Roman forces finally drove Pyrrhus out of Italy and captured Tarentum. Rome now owned or controlled almost all of the Italian peninsula.

A Powerful State Emerges

During its drive to conquer all the lands on the Italian peninsula, the Romans showed both brutality and practicality. At times, the Roman legions massacred enemy civilians and the army took thousands of slaves—a common practice in the ancient world. But Rome's fair treatment of most of its defeated enemies provided for good relations in the future. Extending Roman citizenship and letting cities keep local control led to loyalty toward Rome. The people of the Italian peninsula saw Roman rule or alliances as less threatening than coming under the control of other major powers in the region. With its various arrangements with defeated enemies and new allies, Rome created peace within its borders and developed a source of soldiers and money for future military efforts. Its access to trade markets and natural resources also grew. The years of growth in the Italian peninsula laid the foundation for future expansion.

These years of the Republic also saw important military developments. The Romans built their first major roads as highways for moving troops in any kind of weather. The roads were paved with stones, pebble, or gravel. The roads had a slight hump in the middle so rainwater would drain off to the sides. The earliest major highway was the Appian Road, built

THE MUNICIPA

As it conquered its former Latin allies, Rome gave many of them a large level of local control, and their people received the full rights of Roman citizenship. For the non-Latin peoples it defeated, Rome created a special form of citizenship that included many rights and obligations (including a duty to serve in the military and pay taxes), but not the right to vote. This class of citizenship was known as *civitas sine suffragio*—"citizenship without suffrage." In either case, Rome called these defeated cities *municipia*, which came from the Latin word for "duty," *munus*. Today, towns and cities are sometimes called municipalities, and *municipal* refers to local government affairs or officials.

An Ancient "Tank"

Pyrrhus's invading force included 20 elephants equipped for battle—the first time the Romans had seen these immense beasts. Indian armies were the first to use elephants in battle. They served several military purposes: They could carry huge amounts of supplies, and during a siege they could pull down or batter walls and gates. In an open field, a charging elephant would frighten the enemy's horses and trample troops that could not get out of their path. They also provided a moving shield against enemy troops. At times, armies put wooden towers on the elephants' backs. From there, archers could fire at the enemy troops. In this sense, the war elephants served as "tanks" for ancient armies. Ancient Romans, however, wrote that their troops had some effective anti-tank weapons, including another animal: the pig. A pig's squeal was said to frighten elephants and force them to retreat.

around 312 B.C.E. Without a paved road, an army could get bogged down in mud; using the new roads to move goods and civilians was a secondary concern.

The Romans also continued to learn military tactics and borrow weapons from their enemies. The Samnite Wars gave the army its first experience fighting in the mountains, and the troops began to use javelins similar to the ones the Samnites used. In general, Roman soldiers were better equipped than ever, and almost constant warfare sharpened their skills. Roman soldiers were still citizens fighting for their homeland, not professional warriors. Still, they showed tremendous discipline. They also believed, based on Roman religious teachings, that their wars were blessed by the gods.

Rome, some historians say, also had geography and luck on its side as it grew. With its central location on the Italian peninsula, the Republic could easily move its troops to face an attack in any direction. Rome and its neighboring lands also had fertile fields that provided plenty of food crops. Rome's enemies lacked its geographic advantages and had their own problems. The strongest enemies, such as the Etruscans, sometimes argued among themselves and did not attack as a united force. And when Gaul invaded Rome in 390 B.C.E., its decision to leave was based partly on outside events. Who knows how the history of Rome might have changed if the Gallic invaders had remained in the city.

Overseas Expansion

In 264 B.C.E., Rome began the first of a series of wars with Carthage, its first overseas foe. Carthage controlled a large strip of North Africa along the Mediterranean coast, as well as the islands of Sardinia and Corsica and parts of Spain and Sicily. The Carthaginians, like the Romans, had a Hellenized culture. They relied on sea trade for their wealth and had a powerful navy.

Starting as early as 508 B.C.E., Rome and Carthage signed a series of treaties that promoted peaceful trade between the two states. A dispute in Sicily, however, led to war, when some Sicilians in the city of Messana asked for Roman help against Carthage (Messana, now called Messina, is located in the part of Sicily closest to the Italian peninsula). Carthage's involvement there took it beyond the territory it controlled on the island—and close to Greek cities on the Italian peninsula that were allied with Rome.

Roman forces landed on Sicily and pushed the Carthaginians out of Messana. The Romans then continued to fight across Sicily, hoping to claim the island for the empire. Battling Carthage required building a new navy, since the Carthaginians dominated the seas. In a short period of time, Rome assembled a large fleet. The ships were equipped with a special plank that was lowered onto nearby enemy vessels, so Roman soldiers could board and fight the Carthaginians hand-to-hand. For 2,000 years, navies continued to fight this way, using soldiers or marines who joined the sailors on board ships.

On land, Rome took the war to the Carthaginians, invading North Africa in 256 B.C.E. But after a devastating loss, the Romans withdrew and Sicily remained the main battleground. The war dragged on for another 15 years, with Rome barely defeating its enemy. Carthage gave Sicily to Rome and agreed not to send its ships into Roman waters or recruit mercenaries (foreign soldiers hired to fight for another country) from the Italian peninsula. The First Punic War weakened Carthage as a sea power while boosting Rome's naval ability. It also gave Rome its first overseas territory. After winning control of Sicily, Rome soon added Sardinia and Corsica to its empire. The war, however, had cost Rome tens of thousands of troops.

The victory over Carthage removed one threat to Rome—for awhile. But the Romans still faced problems to their north and east. In the 220s B.C.E., they battled pirates from Illyria, a kingdom along the northern Adriatic Sea. Rome won control of parts of this foreign kingdom, but the pirates remained a problem for almost 200 years. Rome also faced another Gallic invasion, as tribes in the northern part of the Italian peninsula moved southward into Roman territory. Rome defeated this invading army and then kept marching, defeating various Gallic tribes in the northern part of the Italian peninsula.

The Second Punic War

As Rome continued to fight enemies, Carthage regained some of its former power and once again challenged its main rival. The Carthaginians ex-

THE RAVEN

The plank the Romans used to board enemy ships had a special feature called the raven, which was a metal spike. The raven drove through the wooden decks on the Carthaginian ships, helping to keep the vessels close to the attacking Roman ships. Using the raven, the Romans won major sea victories in 260 B.C.E. and the following years. The plank with the raven posed a problem, though. At sea, the size and weight of the plank made Roman ships hard to control, especially during storms. After losing many of its warships at sea, the Romans stopped using the boarding plank and the raven.

panded their holdings on the Iberian peninsula, and in 219 B.C.E. Hannibal (247–182 B.C.E.) commanded a Carthaginian army that defeated a Roman ally there. The Romans demanded that Carthage turn over Hannibal so they could punish him. Carthage refused, and the Second Punic War began.

Hannibal, legend goes, had promised his father Hamilcar Barca (d. c. 229 B.C.E.), that he would always consider Rome his chief enemy. Hamilcar had fought the Romans during the First Punic War. As tensions with Rome grew, Hannibal assembled a large army and marched from the Iberian peninsula across what is now southern France into the Italian peninsula. The Carthaginians, their mercenary forces, and their Gallic allies won several victories. Livy, in his History of Rome, wrote that "the loveliest part of Italy was being reduced to ashes and the smoke was rising everywhere from the burning farms." The Carthaginian forces continued to move southward, bypassing Rome as they tried to find new allies. In 216 B.C.E., Roman troops lost their worst battle at Cannae (today it is spelled Canne), and Hannibal eventually took Tarentum.

Rome, however, still had a big advantage: Because the battles were in Roman territory, it could rebuild its army and keep it supplied. Hannibal lacked a navy that could bring supplies from Carthage or the Iberian peninsula and had to rely on what his men could take from the Romans. The Romans also had enough troops to slowly regain lost cities in the Italian peninsula while simultaneously invading the Iberian peninsula. The Roman general Publius Scipio (236–183 B.C.E.) eventually drove the Carthaginians out of the Iberian peninsula, then invaded Carthage's African lands in 204 B.C.E. Hannibal returned to his homeland to fight the Roman invaders, but his forces lost at Zama in modern-day Tunisia two years later. Scipio won the nickname "Africanus" and was Rome's greatest general of that era. With its victories, Rome took control of the Carthaginian territory in the Iberian peninsula and guaranteed its place as the western Mediterranean's major military power.

The Greek Wars

As the Second Punic War came to an end, the Romans came into greater contact with Greek kingdoms to the east. The vast empire of Alexander the Great had broken up into independent city-states and three major dynasties. The Antigonids controlled Macedonia, the Seleucids ruled over a large part of the Middle East from their capital in Syria, and the Ptolemies controlled Egypt. A less-powerful dynasty, the Attalids, ruled a part of Asia

---

A Daring and Skillful General

Hannibal has been called one of the greatest generals of all time. The Greek historian Polybius (c. 200–c. 125 B.C.E.) wrote in *The Histories* that other Carthaginians thought Hannibal was greedy, and the Romans considered him cruel. That reputation led Roman adults to tell their children that unless they behaved, Hannibal would come after them (as reported in Allen Ward's *A History of the Roman Peoples*). But Hannibal won the respect of his troops by enduring the same hardships they did, eating the same food, and often sleeping on the ground. He planned his Roman campaign for two years and won several dazzling victories. His march across the Alps and his victories in the Italian peninsula showed Hannibal's skills as a planner and a leader. Into the 20th century, generals around the world still studied his tactics, especially his victory at Cannae.

Minor called Pergamum, in what is now western Turkey (Asia Minor is a peninsula in western Asia bordered by the Black and Mediterranean Seas). Relations between the different Greek kingdoms and city-states varied, as some kingdoms tried to gain power at their rivals' expense. The Greek conflicts and Rome's desire to protect its own interests in the eastern Mediterranean led to a series of wars in the region.

Even while fighting Carthage, the Romans had started to play an active role in the east. In 219 B.C.E. King Philip V (237–179 B.C.E.) of Macedonia protected a Greek ruler who challenged Roman authority. Rome then sent ships into the region to harass Macedonian allies and army bases. Four years later, Philip signed a treaty with Rome's main foe, Hannibal. Rome then signed treaties with some smaller Greek states in the region, and they fought Philip while Rome battled Hannibal. (This Greek war is known as the First Macedonian War.) As the Second Punic War was coming to an end, Philip tried to expand his holdings around the Aegean Sea, the main body of water near the mainland of Greece and neighboring islands. In 200 B.C.E., Rome declared war on Macedonia, to protect its Greek allies, stop Philip's aggression, and punish him for his earlier alliance with Hannibal.

After defeating the Macedonians in 197 B.C.E., Rome's next Greek opponents were the Seleucids. Under their king, Antiochus III (242–187 B.C.E.), the Seleucids tried to expand their territory. Fighting with several Greek allies, the Romans defeated Antiochus in 190 B.C.E.. Roman troops fought in both Greece and Asia Minor, but they did not remain in those regions. With the Greek wars, Rome did not acquire new territory, but it did expect the Greek communities to follow Roman orders. Rome also gained from the slaves and riches its soldiers brought home. Rome was asserting itself as the most powerful state in the region, and smaller states feared its power.

Despite Rome's strength, Macedonia once again challenged the Romans, and once again Rome won. After this victory in 168 B.C.E., Rome ended the Antigonid Dynasty and split Macedonia into four separate republics. This marked the first time Rome totally destroyed one of the three Greek kingdoms that traced its roots to Alexander the Great. But even as they defeated the Greeks in battle, the Romans continued to embrace Hellenism.

During the second century B.C.E., Rome was almost constantly at war. In addition to fighting in the east, the Romans battled to secure their control of the Iberian peninsula. They also fought Gallic tribes in the north of the Italian peninsula. In those two regions, the Romans took direct con-

MAN AND GOD

The Roman hero during the Second Macedonian War was Titus Quinctius Flamininus (228–174 B.C.E.). A consul, he led the army that won the major battle of the war, and he granted independence to the Greek people under Philip's rule. Some Greek towns worshiped him as a god. He was the first Roman to receive that honor—some of the later Roman emperors, such as Augustus and Tiberius, were also worshiped as gods by citizens of the eastern part of the empire.

The Roman Dictator

Today the word *dictator* is used in a general way to describe any leader who has complete control over others and uses power ruthlessly. To the Romans, however, a dictator originally had a clearly defined rule. During the monarchy, a king might name a *magister populi*—master of the army—to command his troops for him. Later, under the Republic, elected officials could choose to give this master's power to a person called a *dictator*. During a military or political crisis, the dictator held *imperium* for up to six months.

One legendary dictator was Cincinnatus. In 458 B.C.E., he left his farm to accept the dictator's power and help Rome defeat an enemy army. After 16 days, Cincinnatus returned to his farm. After the American Revolution, some American soldiers founded the Society of Cincinnati, named for this Roman who fought for his nation during a crisis, then returned to his civilian life. A city in Ohio also takes its name from this Roman dictator.

trol of territory. Unlike the Greeks, the various western tribes did not have established political and social systems that the Romans could easily influence—and be influenced by. To preserve its military gains and keep control, Rome had to leave troops behind and set up its own political systems.

In the northern part of the Italian peninsula, a few Gallic tribes were wiped out by the fighting; most survived and became part of the growing Roman republic. The Republic also set up new colonies in the region, as it had done years before in the southern part of the peninsula. The Romans had a tougher time fighting in the Iberian peninsula. Some of the local tribes, such as the Celtiberians, fought in small groups that staged sneak attacks against the Roman forces. (The Celtiberians were a mixture of the Celtic tribes who settled in the Iberian peninsula and the native Iberian people.) The local fighters struck quickly, then fled into the mountains or countryside—a tactic that is now called guerrilla warfare. Rome spent more than 70 years trying to assert its control over the Celtiberians and other native Iberian peoples, finally winning a major victory in 133 B.C.E. Even then, it took several more decades for Rome to secure total rule over the Iberian peninsula.

The Romans also fought one last Punic War. During the second century B.C.E., Carthage regained some of its former strength, as it was still a major trading power in the Mediterranean. The Carthaginians, however, could not hold off the neighboring African kingdom of Numidia. The Numidians took advantage of their friendship with Rome to seize territory from Carthage. Around 150 B.C.E., the Carthaginians finally fought back, even though this military action violated their earlier peace treaty with Rome. The Numidians then turned to Rome for aid.

In the Senate, a well-known official named Cato the Elder (234–149 B.C.E.) supported the Numidians. He had fought the Carthaginians during the Second Punic War and still detested them. For several years, he ended every speech he made by saying, "Carthage must be destroyed" (as quoted in Barlett's Quotations). Cato led the effort to battle Carthage once again.

This time, however, the Carthaginians did not have the will for a long war. They knew Rome's military would crush them. The Carthaginians surrendered without a fight and accepted Rome's surrender terms. But when the Romans demanded that the entire city of Carthage be moved inland, away from the shore, the Carthaginians refused. As sailors and sea traders, their lives depended on being close to the water. Their resistance led to the Third Punic War. When it ended in 146 B.C.E., the Romans followed Cato the Elder's demand and completely destroyed the city. Rome then took control of Carthage's lands, which became the Roman province of Africa.

Marius and Sulla

Only a few decades later, the Romans fought a major war against Numidia. Numidians had aided Rome against Carthage during the Third Punic War. In 112 B.C.E., Jugurtha (d. 104 B.C.E.), the adopted son of the Numidian king, seized power from two rivals with the help of some Roman senators. When the resulting civil war in Numidia disrupted grain supplies to Rome, some Romans called for war. Rome wanted to restore order to make sure it had access to the Numidian grain.

At first the war went badly for Rome, with Jugurtha winning several battles. In 107 B.C.E., a Roman officer named Gaius Marius (157–86 B.C.E.) emerged as a political and military leader. To raise troops to fight Jugurtha, Marius recruited volunteers among the landless peasants. Rome had done this before only during emergencies; Marius made it an accepted practice. These soldiers felt personal loyalty to Marius, and he counted on them to support his political career.

On the battlefield, Marius defeated Jugurtha in 105 B.C.E. The Numidian king was executed using a traditional method for defeated foes—he was strangled. Marius now had a powerful force of fiercely loyal soldiers. He set a pattern that endured for centuries, as popular military commanders relied on loyal troops to help them gain political power. Marius also made the Roman army more professional, improving their weapons and training. A legion now numbered between 5,000 and 6,000 troops, with each soldier carrying a javelin, a sword, and a shield.

MILITARY "MULES"

Under Marius, Roman soldiers began to carry their own basic supplies, such as cooking and building tools, a tent, and enough food for three days. With their heavy backpacks, the soldiers were sometimes known as "Marius's mules."

25

Rome was fairly peaceful for about a decade, until its allies on the Italian peninsula rebelled, demanding full Roman citizenship. At the end of the so-called Social War between Rome and the Italians, the Romans agreed to give their allies full citizenship rights. Rome then turned its attention to the east. King Mithridates VI (132–63 B.C.E.) of Pontus, in Asia Minor, had massacred Romans living in the region and conquered several of the Republic's Greek allies.

Marius wanted to command the army sent to battle Mithridates, but the Senate gave the honor to Lucius Cornelius Sulla (c. 138–78 B.C.E.), who had fought under Marius in North Africa. The two men were rivals, and their rivalry reflected the tensions between Rome's two main political groups: Marius was a *popularis*, one of the politicians who tended to support the interests of the common people; while Sulla sided with the *optimates*, who favored the wealthy and powerful. In 88 B.C.E., after Sulla and his troops left the city, Marius worked with a tribune to pass a law that made Marius commander, replacing Sulla. Fighting broke out in Rome and Sulla returned to the city with some of his troops. For the first time since the founding of the Republic, Romans were waging civil war.

With military support, Sulla won control of the government. He weakened the tribunes' political power while boosting the authority of the Senate and the Centuriate Assembly. He then returned to battle against King Mithridates. While he was gone, Lucius Cornelius Cinna (d. 84 B.C.E.), a consul, tried to overturn the laws Sulla had pushed through. He was driven out of the city but soon recruited Marius to attack Rome. With Marius's help, Cinna emerged as dictator. He died in 84 B.C.E. during a mutiny—a revolt of soldiers against either their officers or civilian authority.

After defeating Mithridates in 85 B.C.E., Sulla returned to the Italian peninsula two years later. He fought two armies sent by the government to stop him from reaching Rome. The general acquired new allies, while his various opponents united against him. Sulla won control of Rome in 82 B.C.E., then had thousands of his enemies tortured and killed. The Centuriate Assembly confirmed his power by making him dictator for life. Sulla set up a government system that favored his wealthy friends and weakened the power of the tribunes. Rome remained at risk for future civil wars, since the plebs and others not connected to Sulla detested his harsh rule. Sulla, wrote Plutarch in his *Lives of Noble Grecians and Romans*, brought "Rome more mischief than all her enemies together had done," by creating so much potential for conflict within the Republic.

The Rise and Fall of Julius Caesar

After Sulla's death in 78 B.C.E., various generals fought for power. Their armies battled foreigners in Iberia and Gaul, and sometimes battled each other as well. Fighting also broke out again in Asia Minor, as Mithridates VI was still trying to extend his influence in the region. During the next several decades, three generals emerged as Rome's main leaders: Pompey the Great (106–48 B.C.E.), Crassus (115–53 B.C.E.), and Julius Caesar. At first, the three men made an informal agreement, called the First Triumvirate, to help each other achieve their political ambitions. But eventually they ended up competing with one another for control of Rome, with Pompey and Caesar the main rivals.

Pompey fought in Iberia and against Mithridates. He and Crassus also ended a slave rebellion in 71 B.C.E. Caesar served as governor of the Iberian peninsula for nine years, where he won several small battles.

Caesar then set out to conquer new territory in central and northern Gaul, fighting German tribes across the Rhine River and making Rome's first entry into the British Isles. Caesar's military operations extended Rome's area of control far to the west and north. With his successes, Caesar emerged as the most powerful general and

CONNECTIONS >>>>>>>>>>>>

All Roads Lead to Rome

Thanks to their talented engineers, the Romans built long, straight roads that lasted for centuries. A few are still used today, and some modern roads follow the same paths that Roman ones did. The Romans had a Latin saying that meant "All roads lead to Rome." This notion was once true, because all major roads started in the center of Rome, like spokes spreading out from the center of a bicycle wheel. The idea also referred to the fact that Rome was the center of the empire, and important decisions were made there. Today, the saying is still used to mean that many different approaches can lead to the same goal, or all paths lead to the same thing.

Roman roads are still found all over Europe. This one leads to the Forum in the old center of Rome.

27

political leader in Rome, and he was eager to assert his strength. He returned to Rome in 49 B.C.E., and the next year he issued orders to cancel the debts of some Romans. The civil wars had created economic chaos, and Caesar's actions led to a slow improvement. Thanks to his military victories and his economic success, Caesar won popular support. By 47 B.C.E., the Senate had twice named him dictator.

During this time, Caesar's troops battled forces loyal to Pompey. The rivalry between the two generals had turned into civil war, with each man hoping to take full control of the Roman government. Battles took place in Iberia and on the Adriatic Sea. Early in 48 B.C.E., Caesar led his troops against Pompey in Greece, winning a victory that forced Pompey to flee to Alexandria, Egypt. The rulers there, Ptolemy XIII (61–48 B.C.E.) and his sister Cleopatra VII (69–30 B.C.E.), killed Pompey, hoping to build an alliance with Caesar.

Soon after, Caesar arrived in Egypt. The Egyptians showed him the severed head of the dead Pompey. Caesar cried for his rival; he did not hate Pompey, he just wanted total power and Pompey had stood in his way.

Caesar then began a famous romance with Cleopatra. He also angered some powerful Egyptians by declaring Roman rule over Egypt and demanding they repay debts owed to Rome. Caesar had to fight the Egyptians to assert his control over the country. After several more quick victories in the east, Caesar made a statement about Egypt that is still quoted today in many contexts: *Veni Vidi Veci*—"I came, I saw, I conquered."

When Caesar returned to Rome in 46 B.C.E., the city greeted him as a hero. He had shown his skills on the battlefield and added to Rome's glory. The senators made him a dictator for 10 years—later extended to life—and gave him other important political positions. These powers made Caesar Rome's first

Crossing the Rubicon

In 49 B.C.E., Julius Caesar faced a major decision in his drive for control of the Roman Empire. He needed to return to Rome to declare himself a candidate for the consulship. At the same time, his opponents in the Senate wanted to take away his army and give more power to Pompey. At the Rubicon River, Caesar made the most important decision of his life—and one that shaped the future of Rome. The Rubicon marked part of the boundary between Cisalpine Gaul, which Caesar governed, and the Roman Republic. Under Roman law, a general could not bring his troops from his provincial territory into the republic. Caesar knew, however, that if he did not invade he would be defeated. He crossed the Rubicon with just one legion and some foreign allies, on his way to winning complete control of the republic, and then the empire. Today, someone who "crosses the Rubicon" makes a crucial decision with results that cannot be changed.

emperor, although he refused to accept the title. As Plutarch describes it in his biography of Caesar, the Romans hoped that "the government of a single person would give them time to breathe after so many civil wars and calamities."

Caesar's coup—overthrowing a 500-year-old democracy—is perhaps one of the most studied and controversial revolutions in history. In his own time, and in ours, he was viewed by some as a great military and political leader and by others as a man who would stop at nothing to get and keep power. No one can deny the enormous changes in Rome that Caesar and his allies wrought. The political culture of Rome was changed forever, and many political freedoms were permanently lost.

CONNECTIONS >>>>>>>>>>>

Triumphs and Ovations

Successful Roman generals earned public acclaim in Rome. In a tradition dating back to the Etruscans, some winning generals, called *triumphators*, were awarded a high honor known as a triumph. They paraded into the city on a chariot covered in a thin layer of gold, with four horses pulling it down the streets. (A chariot is a two-wheeled cart driven while standing.) Behind them marched magistrates, soldiers, and prisoners. The celebration ended with the execution of prisoners at a temple. For less important victories, generals were given an *ovatio*, or ovation. In this simpler procession, a victorious general rode into Rome on horseback. Today, an ovation, or public applause, is still used to honor great achievements.

Caesar tried to give the peoples of the Italian peninsula more equality with the Romans and strengthen Rome's rule over its other lands. He also sent former soldiers and other citizens to new colonies overseas. Building the new colonies provided jobs and homes for the returning troops and brought Roman influence to foreign lands. Many of the new towns he founded still exist today, including Seville in Spain, Arles in France, and Geneva in Switzerland. Caesar also gave Roman citizenship to a large group of provincial residents who moved to Rome. Under Caesar, Rome was truly becoming an international empire. The formal founding of the empire, however, would not come for several more years.

CHAPTER 2

The Empire at Its Peak

CAESAR'S "LIFETIME" RULE AS DICTATOR DID NOT LAST LONG. He had many enemies in the Senate, and in March 44 B.C.E. they united to assassinate him. The assassins included officers who had served under Caesar in Gaul but were angered by his overthrow of the Roman Republic. As the Roman historian Suetonius describes it in his *Twelve Caesars*, "Confronted by a ring of drawn daggers, [Caesar] drew the top of his gown over his face. . . . Twenty-three dagger thrusts went home as he stood there." The assassins hoped to bring back the old Republic. Instead Caesar's death sparked another civil war, as once again several men competed for power.

Trying to bring back the Republic, many historians believe, was doomed to fail. The empire had grown too large for a republican government to defend itself against outside enemies and to control upheavals within its borders. It needed a strong, centralized government, such as the one Caesar tried to build. And too many nobles eager for power and wealth had seen that a single man, with military support, could take over the government, even if the forms of the old republican system remained. These ambitious men would continue to find ways to seize control.

Three Men Vie to Be Emperor

Three men with ties to Caesar emerged to compete for his position. Marc Antony (c. 83–30 B.C.E.) had been one of Caesar's trusted aides. Lepidus (d. c. 12 B.C.E.) had served in Caesar's government. The third man was the only one with family ties: Octavian was Caesar's grandnephew, and in his will Caesar also adopted him as his son. Just 19 years old at the time, Octavian thought he had the best claim to power. He also had many powerful supporters in the Senate.

OPPOSITE
The Ruins of Pompeii
In 79, the volcano Mount Vesuvius erupted, burying several cities, including Pompeii, a seaside resort near Rome. The ash preserved the city in remarkable condition, and archaeologists have learned much about life in ancient Rome from studying Pompeii.

Caesar's dramatic and bloody death may be the most famous political assassination in world history. Thanks to the writings of Roman historians and the English playwright William Shakespeare (1564–1616), people today still know the phrase, "Beware the Ides of March." According to Suetonius and Plutarch, an augur—a person who reads signs in nature to predict the future—had warned Caesar something terrible would happen on the Ides, which is the 15th of the month. Caesar was, in fact, murdered on that day.

The records of the assassination also suggest that Caesar spoke his last words to a former friend who turned against him. One of the leaders of the assassins was Brutus (c. 85–42 B.C.E.). Caesar supposedly said to him in Greek, "You too, Brutus my son?" In his play about Caesar, Shakespeare presents the phrase in Latin as, "*Et tu, Brute?*" That version is still sometimes used today by people who feel they have been betrayed by someone they trusted.

In 43 B.C.E. Octavian battled forces led by Antony, who shortly afterward teamed up with Lepidus. The three men then decided to rule together, forming what was called the Second Triumvirate. Each ruled part of the empire on his own. The triumvirs still faced enemies, as two of Caesar's assassins, Brutus and Cassius (d. 42 B.C.E.), commanded legions in the east. After defeating them, each triumvir tried to gain total control at the expense of his partners. Lepidus gradually lost influence, leaving Octavian and Antony in a struggle for power.

At first Antony was stronger, but he lost support when he began focusing his attention on Egypt and his relationship with its queen, Cleopatra. Octavian, meanwhile, gained important allies in the Italian peninsula, including army veterans and people who had supported Caesar. Octavian also won popularity after ending a military threat against the Italian peninsula from Sextus Pompey, an old enemy of Caesar and the Triumvirate.

By 36 B.C.E., Octavian controlled the western part of the empire and Antony the east. Their struggle to control the entire empire ended five years later when Octavian's naval forces defeated Antony's fleet, which included ships supplied by Cleopatra. By 29 B.C.E., Octavian returned to Rome as the supreme ruler. The official Roman Empire, with him as the first emperor, was about to begin.

The Reign of Augustus

Augustus's official titles and powers changed over time, but no one doubted who ruled Rome. Unlike Julius Caesar, Augustus chose to work with the Senate. He gained his power legally, rather than by military might, as he won elections for the consulship and the Senate granted him the powers of a tribune. He also earned the title *princeps civitatis*, or "first man of the state." This honor had sometimes been awarded during the Republic. The old Republic, however, was clearly gone, because Augustus had wealth and military power no other Roman or foreign ruler in the Mediterranean could match. Romans, for the most part, accepted his rule because they were tired of civil war and because Augustus did not act like a tyrant.

Thanks to his military victory over Antony and Cleopatra, Augustus added Egypt to Rome's territory and great riches to his personal wealth. With that money and other war booty, he rebuilt important public buildings in the capital city. In his *Res Gestae*, an account of his rule, Augustus wrote, "Eighty-two temples in the city in my sixth consulship [28 B.C.E.] with the authority of the Senate I repaired, passing over none which at that time ought to have been repaired" (as quoted in Robert Sherk's *Translated*

Documents of Greece and Rome). The emperor also used his own funds to pay soldiers' bonuses and establish new colonies. These included settlements in Africa, Sicily, Iberia, Macedonia, and Gaul.

After 27 B.C.E., Augustus had direct control over several Roman provinces: the Iberian peninsula (which was actually two separate provinces), Gaul, Syria, and Egypt. He appointed the officials who ran local affairs, and he could decide how to use the troops stationed there. The Senate ruled the other provinces, appointing the officials who ruled in its name. Still, Augustus could overrule these local officials when he chose.

Under Augustus Rome entered a largely peaceful era, especially in the Italian peninsula. The chaos of the late Republic was over and the economy improved. When the economy weakened, Augustus made sure everyone could at least afford wheat. Augustus also tried to improve Roman morals. He promoted marriage, punished people who had sexual relations outside of marriage, and tried to end bribery. In today's terms, Augustus might be called a conservative, someone who valued law and order and traditional standards of behavior.

The Battle at Actium
Italian Antonio Vassilacchi (1556–1629) painted this scene of Marc Antony's defeat in Egypt on the walls of the Villa Barbarigo just outside Venice.

33

A Young and Attractive Queen

Cleopatra was 21 years old when she first had direct contact with Roman rulers. With her intelligence and beauty, she charmed Julius Caesar, who was some 30 years older than she. They began a relationship that lasted for several years. Cleopatra had a son during this time and said Caesar was the father. After Caesar's death, Cleopatra began a love affair and political alliance with Marc Antony. The queen's involvement with Antony and Roman politics played a part in the rise of Octavian as the first emperor, because many Romans did not like the idea of a foreign queen influencing their affairs.

In 1607 William Shakespeare wrote about Cleopatra's relations with Antony in his play *Antony and Cleopatra*. About 300 years later, the Irish playwright George Bernard Shaw (1856–1950) wrote a work called *Caesar and Cleopatra*. Both plays are still performed today, showing the continued interest in these powerful ancient figures. Today, Cleopatra represents many things. She is seen as a symbol of a strong and independent woman. She also represents the dangers of love for ambitious men who choose the wrong partners. Her death, a suicide from the bite of a poisonous snake, has often been shown in paintings.

When Augustus sent troops into battle, they focused on extending Rome's rule over foreign people or preserving control where it already ruled. Augustus extended the empire's borders in the Iberian peninsula, Gaul, Germany, the Middle East, and Asia Minor. He also created alliances with other kingdoms that wanted to avoid war with the Roman Empire. Modern historians sometimes call these allies client states or client kingdoms.

By the time of his death in 14 C. E., Augustus was known as the *pater patriae*– "father of his country"–another title Romans had granted in earlier times. Suetonius, in his *Twelve Caesars*, reports that the emperor wept when he received that honor, saying, "Fathers of the Senate, I have at last achieved my highest ambition." In many parts of the empire he was worshiped as a religious figure. Augustus, who was loyal to the traditional Roman gods, did not like the idea of being deified–turned into a god. After his death, however, the Senate officially declared Augustus a god.

The Empire After Augustus

Neither Julius Caesar nor Augustus wanted to be called a king, and Romans did not call their new form of government a monarchy. Romans still had bad memories of their last experience with monarchs (see page 16).

Still, the first two caesars had clearly established a strong central state under the ultimate command of one person, despite Augustus's attempts to preserve the Republic's traditional political bodies.

Under a monarchy, a relative—typically the oldest son—takes over when the ruler dies. Power is automatically passed on within the same family, creating what is called a dynasty. Augustus claimed his powers under Rome's constitution—the written laws and accepted traditions that described the form and process of government. Those powers came from the vote of the people, in their various assemblies. Still, Augustus could choose who would take over as emperor when he died, and he preferred to keep the power within his family. The Senate, however, would have to approve the choice. No Roman emperor could guarantee that he could create a family dynasty.

Augustus did not have any sons, so at first he considered passing on his authority to one of his grandsons. He eventually named his stepson, Tiberius (42 B.C.E.–37 C.E.), as his choice to succeed him. He indicated his preference for the first time in 4 C.E. by asking that Tiberius be voted the same constitutional powers for a 10-year period as Augustus himself held. The vote was repeated in 14 C.E., just before Augustus' death.

On the whole, Tiberius followed Augustus's example and concentrated on strengthening Rome's control over the lands it already ruled, ending revolts in Gaul, Thrace (a province in the Balkans), and North Africa. Once again, to aid the mobility of its troops, Rome built new roads. This time the government focused on some of the outer edges of the empire. The new roads also helped local farmers and merchants, boosting the economy in those regions.

CONNECTIONS >>>>>>>>>>>>

Names of an Emperor

At birth, Octavian was called Gaius Octavius. After his uncle's death he changed his name to Gaius Julius Caesar Octavanius, although modern historians refer to him as Octavian during this time of his life. Shortly after he became emperor, Octavian was given the title Augustus, which in Latin means something blessed or approved of by the augurs. He was the first Roman person to receive that title. Augustus also had a month named for him, which in English became August. In English, the word august also refers to something that is majestic or royal and deserves respect.

Augustus's title of *princeps civitatis* was often shortened to *princeps*. The form of government created by Augustus was called a *principate* (which means rule by an imperial emperor, while still retaining some institutions from the Republic, such as the Senate). The English word *prince* comes from *princeps*, as does *principality*, the land ruled by a prince.

Tiberius was good at overseeing the daily workings of the government, or choosing skilled people to do it for him. As a ruler, however, he was not popular. By nature, Tiberius was somewhat shy, a loner who sometimes slipped into bouts of depression. He did not spend lavishly on buildings and public festivals, as Augustus had. Tiberius also tried to weaken the Senate's power and limit free speech in Rome. People accused of spreading rumors about the emperor faced trial. If convicted, they were executed for treason.

In 26, Tiberius moved to the island of Capri, off the western coast of the Italian peninsula. He still made major decisions, but officials in Rome carried out day-to-day affairs. One of Tiberius's most important aides in Rome was Sejanus (d. 31), the head of the Praetorian Guard, a special branch of the military that protected the emperor. Sejanus first tried to eliminate anyone who might be a threat to Tiberius, having them killed or sent into exile. By 31, Tiberius realized that Sejanus hoped to take over the government himself, and the emperor ordered soldiers in Rome to execute Sejanus and his family. The emperor also killed Romans who had supported Sejanus in his quest for power.

Tiberius died in 37, and members of the Praetorian Guard then declared Caligula (12–41) the next emperor. He was the great-grandson of Augustus and the son of Germanicus (15 B.C.E.–19 C. E.), who had been a popular general and a member of the royal family, and who was poisoned by a political enemy.

Caligula's real name was Gaius Julius Caesar Germanicus. *Caligula*, Latin for "little boots," was a nickname he earned as a boy. He spent time with his father's troops in Germany, and his mother often dressed him as a Roman soldier. The uniform included replicas of the leather boots the soldiers wore, which were called *caligae*.

At first, Caligula offered hope for ending the worst of Tiberius's changes. The new emperor restored some constitutional practices that Tiberius had abolished—for example, he restored the right of the assemblies to elect some magistrates—and he tried to improve relations with the Senate. Caligula also spent money on grand public games and festivals, which were very popular with the common people.

After a few years, however, it became clear that Caligula suffered from a mental illness. He spent all the money Tiberius left him on lavish public festivals and personal excesses, and had to raise taxes. He insulted the Senate and began to see himself as a king. Caligula tried to eliminate any rivals to himself and his family by falsely accusing them of treason and

AN UNOFFICIAL DYNASTY

Augustus belonged to the *gens*, or clan, known as Julian. Tiberius's gens was the Claudian. The next three emperors after him had ties to both clans. Together, the first four emperors after Augustus are often called the Julio-Claudian Dynasty, even though imperial power was not automatically passed on within the family, as in a monarchy. Some future emperors were also able to create dynasties.

having them executed. Some of the people he considered enemies he forced to commit suicide. Caligula also demanded that Romans worship him as a living god.

By 41, leading Roman citizens decided they had to end Caligula's rule, and they assassinated him. The assassins also killed the emperor's wife and daughter, to make sure they would never play a role in imperial politics.

Once again the Praetorian Guard selected the next emperor. They made an unlikely choice, picking Caligula's uncle, Claudius. Brother of the popular Germanicus, Claudius had struggled with physical problems his whole life and had difficulty speaking clearly. These defects convinced some Romans that Claudius was mentally ill as well. The new emperor, however, actually had a sharp mind. He also had good political skills, and promised the guards money if they supported him as emperor.

Like Tiberius and Caligula, Claudius sometimes had bad relations with the Senate. But he was popular with average Romans, as he spent money on public buildings and lowered some taxes.

Claudius also made the first major expansion of Roman territory since Augustus. In the east Rome took complete control of Thrace, and the empire began to play a role in nearby Dacia, in what is now Romania. Roman activity spread all along the Black Sea and reached as far as the Don River, in what is now Russia. In North Africa Claudius strengthened Roman rule over Mauretania, modern-day Morocco and part of Algeria. In the Middle East, Rome annexed a former client kingdom, Judaea.

The main expansion of the empire under Claudius came in Britain. Some Roman culture had spread to the British Isles after Julius Caesar invaded Britain about 100 years before. Rome, however, did not have direct control of Britain, and some of the native kings posed a threat to Rome's allies there. In 43 Roman troops defeated the main opposition king, then won the loyalty of 11 other local kings. Over the next several years Claudius created a province in Britain, which continued to grow after his death.

Notorious Emperor
This 1596 anonymous Italian engraving shows Caligula. The emperor began his reign with promising reforms, but it ended when he was assassinated after it became clear he had gone mad.

Claudius died in 51. Ancient sources say he was poisoned by his wife, but modern historians are not so sure. In any event, his stepson Nero (37–68) took over as emperor, once again with the support of the Praetorian Guard. As Nero came to power, Rome faced trouble in the east, as it competed with the distant kingdom of Parthia (in what is now Iran) to control Armenia. From 55 to 61, Nero also had to confront a bloody rebellion in Britain. At home the emperor sometimes battled with the patricians and the Senate.

In 64 a huge fire spread through Rome, destroying half of the city. Nero was away from Rome when the blaze began, but he quickly returned and to the city and tried to ease the suffering caused by the fire. He set up shelters for the homeless and brought extra food into the city. Rumors soon spread, however, that he had ordered the fire set so he would have an excuse to rebuild the city in a grand style. Nero did spend huge sums to rebuild, especially his own palace. To raise money, he took away lands from some wealthy provincial citizens and raised some taxes.

In Judaea, Nero's actions, as well as many local issues (for example, Roman officials did not punish some Greeks who had attacked a group of Jews in a nearby city), led to a rebellion in 66. Two years later another revolt broke out in Gaul, and some of Nero's provincial governors had begun to turn against him. By 68 Nero was forced out of power. He ordered a servant to kill him before his foes could murder him. Nero could not bring himself

CONNECTIONS >>>>>>>>>>>>>

A Holy Province

The Roman province of Judaea was at the center of what had been the ancient Jewish state of Israel. Under Roman rule, Judaea started as client state, was annexed by Augustus in the year 6, then was made a client state again until Claudius reannexed it in 44.

The Jewish population of Judaea rebelled in 66, and again in 132, during Hadrian's reign. In one of their bloodiest campaigns in the region, the Romans killed perhaps 500,000 people in the process of restoring order. The Romans then forced all the Jews out of Jerusalem, their former capital, and the province's name was changed to Syria Palestina. Palestina is Latin for "land of the Philistines." In the Old Testament of the Bible, the Philistines were enemies of the ancient Israelites, the first Jewish people in the region. Today Palestinians are Arabs who live primarily in Israel and Jordan. Many want to create an independent nation of Palestine in the Middle East.

Today, to the world's Christians, Judaea is best known as the homeland of Jesus Christ, who was born during the reign of Augustus and died during Tiberius's rule. Muslims also trace the roots of their faith, Islam, to the region, and Judea is the location of the modern Jewish state of Israel. Because of its importance to Christians, Jews, and Muslims, what was once Judaea is sometimes called the Holy Land.

to commit suicide, something patrician Romans did to keep their honor in the face of personal defeats.

The Four Emperors and the Flavians

Nero's death began a chaotic year in Roman politics, as four different men briefly took control of the government. In the first book of his *Histories*, Tacitus (c. 56–c. 107) wrote that the era was "rich in disasters, frightful in its wars, torn by civil strife, and even in peace full of horrors." Finally, Vespasian (9–79) won the backing of the Senate and restored order to the empire. He also founded the Flavian Dynasty, named for his *gens*, Flavius.

Spoils of War
This relief from the Arch of Titus in Rome was erected in the Forum in 81 by the emperor Domitian to commemorate Titus's sack of Jerusalem following a rebellion there. Roman soldiers carry off treasures from the Jewish Temple.

A member of the *equites* and a successful general, Vespasian ended revolts across the empire. He also reformed the army, taking in new recruits from Gaul and the Iberian peninsula and having more legions serve far from the lands where they lived. This reduced the risk of local politicians winning support from the legions and trying to undercut Rome's authority.

In general, Vespasian tried to tie the western provinces more closely to Rome, so the people in those regions would identify with the empire and not with local concerns. He focused on strengthening the Roman Empire, rather than maintaining its existing borders. His sons Titus (39–81) and Domitian (51–96) largely continued this policy.

Although Vespasian and Titus were mostly well liked, Domitian made many enemies in the Senate, because he gave the *equites* and more non-Italians greater influence in the government. The emperor also exiled or killed some senators who opposed him. In addition, Domitian faced a revolt from a general commanding troops in Germany. Despite all these problems, though, on the whole Domitian and the other Flavian emperors did a good job of restoring order in Rome and preserving the empire's strength.

The Fire and the Fiddler

Nero fancied himself a talented musician. He played the lyre, a small stringed instrument, while singing in a voice Suetonius describes as "feeble." In *The Twelve Caesars*, Suetonius goes on to say that when Nero gave public performances, the audience was prevented from leaving. As the historian satirically wrote, "We read of women in the audience giving birth and of men so bored . . . that they . . . shammed dead and were carried away for burial."

When the great fire broke out in Rome, Nero—according to Suetonius—sang a song. The singer would have been playing his lyre as well. Over the centuries, the legend developed that Nero fiddled while Rome burned. Modern historians do not think the story is true. Still, people who refuse to take action during an obvious crisis are sometimes said to be fiddling while Rome burns, just as Nero supposedly did.

The Five Good Emperors

The Flavian Dynasty ended in 96 when Domitian was murdered by some senators and members of the imperial court. The plotters probably included the emperor's wife. She and others watched as Domitian executed a cousin that he believed opposed his rule; the assassins feared they might become the emperor's next targets. With Domitian gone, the senators then chose one of their own, Nerva (30–98), to take power. His reign marks the start of a long period of stability in the Roman Empire. Later historians called Nerva and the four rulers after him the five good emperors. During the 18th century, British historian Edward Gibbon wrote the famous book *The Decline and Fall of the Roman Empire*, in which he said the rule of these five men marked "the period in the history of the world during which the condition of the human race was most happy and prosperous" (as quoted in Hooper's book). Gibbon, however, was defining the human race narrowly, referring only to the people who benefited from Rome's rule.

When Domitian died, the senators considered several factors as they chose a new emperor. At age 66, Nerva was not apt to live long enough to cause any real problems. He also did not have any children, so he would not be able to found a dynasty. And as one of their own, Nerva was not likely to grab power from the Senate. The new emperor, however, did not have strong support from the Praetorian Guard, who could still play a role in ending one emperor's reign and choosing another. Nerva decided to strengthen his position by adopting a well-respected military leader as his son. He chose Trajan (53–117).

Born in Iberia, Trajan became the first Roman emperor who came from the provinces. After Trajan came to power in 98, he won the support of the common people, the Senate, and the army. At home Trajan strengthened a program that aided the poor children of the Italian peninsula, and he spent money to improve public buildings and roads in the provinces. Trajan is best remembered, however, for carrying out several military campaigns that led to the last major expansion of the Roman Empire's borders.

In 101 the Roman army invaded Dacia. The empire's relation with the kingdom there had been shaky since Domitian's reign. Trajan wanted to make sure Dacia acknowledged Rome's rule. With its defeat in 102, Dacia once again became a client state. Three years later, however, the Dacians challenged Rome's dominance. Trajan returned to the kingdom, won a decisive victory, and made Dacia a province of the empire. The emperor then sent Roman soldiers to live in the region, while taking 50,000 Dacians as slaves.

A few years later Trajan turned to the east, clashing with the kingdom of Parthia. For decades the Romans and Parthians had battled for influence over Armenia, which lay between Parthia and Rome's eastern provinces. In 115 Trajan captured the Parthian capital and claimed several new provinces in what is now Iran and Iraq. These new lands included Armenia, Mesopotamia, and Assyria (the last two are in present-day Iraq). Rome, however, could not hold onto all its new possessions; the Parthians regained their military strength and revolts broke out in some of these eastern lands. When Trajan died in 117, Rome was already beginning to lose control in the region.

Before he died, Trajan seems to have adopted Hadrian (76–138), one of his generals in the east,

CONNECTIONS >>>>>>>>>>>>

Buried History

In 79, the year Titus became emperor, Rome faced one of the worst natural disasters in its history. Near Naples, the volcano Mount Vesuvius erupted, destroying several towns, including Pompeii and Herculaneum.

The area was popular with wealthy Romans, who built summer homes overlooking the Bay of Naples. When Vesuvius erupted, it covered the homes, local businesses, and many residents with a thick layer of ash and rock. Pliny the Younger (c. 61–c. 113), a Roman politician and writer, was a teenager at the time. He and his mother escaped the eruption. In a letter to Tacitus, quoted in *Roman Realities* by Finley Hooper, Pliny recalled hearing "the shrieks of women, the wailing of infants and the shouting of men." He also described the scene: "…darkness came on once more and ashes began to fall again, this time in heavy showers. We rose from time to time and shook them off, otherwise we should have been buried and crushed beneath their weight."

For hundreds of years, Pompeii and Herculaneum were forgotten, buried by the volcano's blast. Then, starting in the 16th century, Italians began to find traces of the two cities. Today, parts of Pompeii and Herculaneum have been excavated, revealing what life was like in the Roman Empire in 79. Visitors can walk stone-paved streets, explore homes, and imagine the sights and sounds that once filled these bustling cities.

CONNECTIONS >>>>>>>>>>>>

Rome's Arabia

During the second war with Dacia, Rome also acquired a new province in the Middle East—Arabia, in what is now part of Egypt and Israel. The province's name came from the Latin word for the native people of the region, *Arab*. The Latin word was based on the Greek *Arap*. Today, the name Arabia appears in the name of the oil-rich Arab kingdom of Saudi Arabia.

although modern historians lack solid proof. (Adoption was not limited to orphan children. An emperor might adopt a favorite general in order to make him a part of the royal family and a possible successor.) Hadrian also had some family ties to the emperor. At Trajan's death the eastern troops declared their support for Hadrian as emperor, and the Senate agreed. Hadrian realized that Trajan's conquests were too difficult to defend and gave up all the lands Rome had won from Parthia that it had not already lost, although the empire still had some control in Armenia.

Hadrian focused on strengthening the empire's old borders, particularly in Britain. He had a wall built that kept out invading tribes from the north (see page 11). He also dealt with several revolts in the existing provinces. Once he restored order, Hadrian traveled throughout the empire and supervised the building or rebuilding of temples, public baths, and theaters. During his travels he stressed improving discipline among the troops on the frontier. In Rome, the emperor appointed the best people he could find to run the empire's daily affairs. Often in the past, emperors chose friends and relatives for government jobs, and they tried to do as little work as possible. But Hadrian's government employees had to be both skilled and loyal, and the emperor expected them to act as professionals.

The fourth of the "good emperors," Antoninus Pius (86–161), was also the founder of a new imperial dynasty, the Antonines. Hadrian adopted Antoninus after his first adopted son died. The emperor told leading senators (as quoted by Michael Grant in *The Antonines*) that his new son was "neither young enough to do anything reckless nor so old as to neglect anything." Seeing how well Hadrian had done by reforming government operations, Antoninus did not make any major changes. He also did not pursue any foreign wars and continued to improve Roman defenses against outside threats. Rome enjoyed peace within its borders as well.

While Hadrian was still alive, he ordered Antoninus to also adopt two sons. One of them was Marcus Aurelius (121–180), who became emperor in 161. Well educated and a philosopher of note, Marcus Aurelius was also a skilled general, and he led Rome through several military challenges. In the east, Parthia invaded Armenia and Syria. In the west, Germanic tribes stormed across the Danube River. Marcus Aurelius took direct control of the fighting with the Germans, which began in 168. The Germanic tribes won several early victories and drove deep into Roman territory before Marcus Aurelius finally organized defenses that drove them back across the Danube. Rome eventually claimed new territory in Eastern Europe, although it did not hold this territory for long. A few years later the Romans battled the Germans along the Danube again. Marcus Aurelius died in 180 during this military campaign.

Marcus Aurelius was the last of the five good emperors. After him came Commodus (161–193), his natural son and the last of the Antonines. Historian Michael Grant, in *The Antonines*, quotes Roman historian Cassius Dio (150–235) describing the new emperor Commodus: "His great simplicity . . . together with his cowardice, made him the slave of his companions, and it was through them that he . . . was led on into lustful and cruel habits, which soon became his second nature." Commodus also spent too much money, hurting Rome's economy, and he offended some senators by participating in the public games, as Nero had done. Romans who supported traditional values thought emperors should not take part in those public festivities.

The Severan Dynasty

The negative feelings about Commodus's behavior spread throughout the imperial court; even his sister joined one plot against him. Commodus later ordered her execution. In 192, however, a second plot succeeded and Commodus was assassinated. For several months the empire was in turmoil, and another civil war erupted. Two men briefly served as emperor, but both were murdered. Septimius Severus (146–211), a general fighting along the Danube, finally emerged as the new emperor and the founder of the Severan Dynasty. After defeating his rivals, Septimius fought briefly with Parthia, adding territory in Mesopotamia, and he also made new gains in Africa. Later in his reign he tried to extend Roman control into Scotland, but the local tribes used guerrilla tactics to drive off the Romans.

Septimius was more of a soldier than a politician, and he counted on the support of his troops to preserve his power. He gave his soldiers raises. The soldiers on the frontier were especially important to him, since the empire faced constant threats from invaders, so he allowed

PAX ROMANA

In his book *Roman Realities,* historian Finley Hooper notes that "the *Pax Romana* was never more secure than during Antoninus' reign." The phrase Pax Romana— "Roman peace"—was often used to describe the long periods during the empire when Rome was not at war, a benefit of its great military strength and alliances with neighboring nations. The Pax Romana was a prosperous time for both the Romans and the foreign people brought into the empire and exposed to Roman culture. Some historians say the Pax Romana lasted from the reign of Augustus through 180, even though those years were not always entirely peaceful.

CONNECTIONS >>>>>>>>>>>>

The Antonines on Film

In 2001, the movie *Gladiator* won the Academy Award for Best Picture. The film was about a fictional Roman general, played by Russell Crowe, but its characters also included Marcus Aurelius and Commodus. The movie showed Commodus's love for the gladiatorial games—combat matches to the death. During the games, gladiators used an assortment of weapons against both animals and one another.

them to marry native women who lived near the frontier forts. Septimius also spent money on building projects in the provinces, trying to balance the amount of attention they received compared to the Italian peninsula.

In Rome Septimius weakened the power of the Senate and tried to guarantee its loyalty to him. He executed some senators who had supported his rivals and brought in new ones from the provinces. A select group of personal advisors who met in council played a larger role in the government, replacing the Senate as the emperor's main group of advisors.

After Septimius's death in 211, his two sons, Geta (189–212) and Caracalla (188–217), briefly ruled as co-emperors, until Caracalla murdered his brother and assumed full control. Like his father, Caracalla spent a lot of time on the battlefield, because Rome faced constant threats from the Germanic tribes and Parthia. The Severan Dynasty was briefly broken in 217, when Macrinus (c. 164–218), a Praetorian prefect (commander of the Praetorian Guards), assassinated Caracalla. The next year, Septimius's sister-in-law, Julia Maesa (d. 226), maneuvered her grandson Elagabalus (203–222) onto the throne, restoring some link to the old dynasty. Spreading the rumor that the boy was the son of Caracalla helped Julia win the army's support for the new emperor.

After four years, a second grandson of Julia Maesa, Severus Alexander (208–235), came to power. He was only 14 years old at the time, and his mother Julia Mamaea (d. 235) and his grandmother actually ran the government. Finley Hooper, in *Roman Realities*, claims that under Alexander, "the affairs of Rome were, for the first and only time, in the hands of women." He also says the two Julias were the best Roman "emperors" since Marcus Aurelius. They turned to the Senate for support and guidance, restoring some of the influence it had lost under Septimius.

During most of the Severan Dynasty the army had been at the center of imperial concerns. Keeping the forces strong—especially on the frontiers—and loyal were the keys to holding on to power. Severus Alexander, however, did not earn the same respect from the troops that

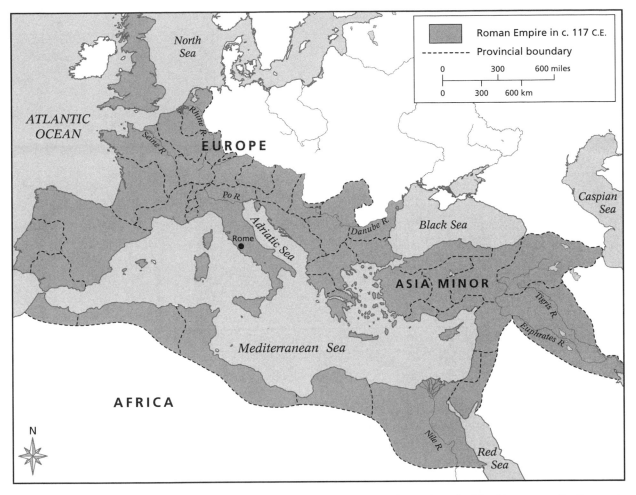

Septimius and Caracalla had. His mother had not given the soldiers the bonuses they had come to expect. Even worse, she and Alexander were ready to give money to Germanic tribes threatening the empire, instead of fighting them. In 235 the Roman troops in Germany revolted, killing both the emperor and his mother.

The end of the Severan Dynasty marked a turning point in Roman history. The country went through 50 years of civil war, with soldiers proclaiming one general after another the emperor. The internal fighting further weakened Rome's borders, leaving the empire open to new attacks. Rome had reached its peak, and it now began a slow decline.

The Empire at Its Largest
The Roman Empire in 117, the year of Trajan's death. The next emperor, Hadrian, realized that Trajan's conquests were too difficult to defend and focused instead on strengthening the empire's old borders.

CHAPTER 3

The Decline and Fall of Rome

THE END OF THE SEVERAN DYNASTY IN 235 INTRODUCED what some historians of Rome have called a period of anarchy (disorder and chaos), with no strong central government in control. For 50 years, a series of generals and politicians claimed the title of emperor, and a separate mini-state with its own emperors rose in Gaul. Parts of the eastern empire also had local rulers for a time. Historians Tim Cornell and John Matthews, in *Atlas of the Roman World*, say the exact number of men who tried to rule all or parts of the empire from 235 to 284 may never be known, but, "Nearly all met violent deaths in civil or foreign wars, or by conspiracy."

Several problems created the anarchy of the age. Rome could no longer afford to field an army large enough to defend all its distant borders. On many sides, barbarian tribes and established kingdoms confronted Roman troops. The Goths, originally from northern Europe, attacked Asia Minor, Germanic tribes moved against Gaul and Spain, and the Sassanid Empire rose in the East. A shortage of precious metals also hurt the Roman economy.

One of the economic problems Rome faced during the third century—inflation—sometimes worries governments today. Inflation refers to the rising cost of goods over time. If wages rise at the same rate as prices, inflation is not a problem. But if wages remain flat or decline, then people cannot afford to buy as much as they could in the past. In Rome, inflation was mostly the result of the government's debasing the money. At one time, silver coins were made completely of silver. Everyone knew how much silver was in a coin and the value of the metal. Debasing the coins—putting less silver in them—meant they had less value. By 260, a "silver" coin was only 5 percent silver; the rest was less valuable metals. People needed more money to buy the same amount of goods they could purchase with the older, more valuable coins. Over a seven-year period starting in 267, prices rose 700 percent.

Under changes made during the Severan Dynasty, Roman soldiers were allowed to marry for the first time, and they often wed local provincial women. Provincial auxiliary troops also played a larger role in the military. With these developments, more soldiers had strong family ties in the regions where they served, and they were reluctant to move and fight in other parts of the empire, as the emperors sometimes demanded. The troops proclaimed their own commanders as emperors, to try to prevent their being repositioned and to focus the government's attention on their region.

Notable Emperors Within the Chaos

In the long list of emperors and supposed emperors during this period, a few stand out. In 253, Valerian (b. c. 193) became emperor, and soon his son Gallienus (c. 218–c. 268) joined him as co-ruler. The father took charge of military actions in the east, while the son focused on the west. Valerian had trouble battling the empires to the east; he was captured some time around 260, leaving Gallienus as the sole emperor. Gallienus then relied on the Roman client state of Palmyra to protect Roman interests in Asia Minor and the Middle East. Still, the Goths won major victories in that part of the empire. Jordanes, a fifth-century historian, wrote in his *History of the Goths*, "While Gallienus was given over to luxurious living of every sort . . . leaders of the Goths . . . sailed across the strait of the Hellespont to Asia. There they laid waste many populous cities and set fire to the renowned temple of Diana. . . ." The invaders then returned to their home in Europe, destroying more cities along the way.

In the west, Gallienus managed to drive out some barbarian tribes who had reached deep into the Italian peninsula. He also fought pirates who sailed off the coasts of Gaul and Britain. As in the east, he relied on a local leader, Postumus (dates unknown), for help. This Roman general had rebelled against Gallienus, but the emperor left him alone to deal with the barbarians who continued to threaten other parts of the western empire. Postumus forced Germanic invaders out of Gaul and successfully defended its borders. Postumus was the first "emperor" of a state within Rome, eventually ruling over Gaul and parts of Spain and Britain. He set up his own senate and minted his own coins.

THE GOTHS

The Goths, a Germanic tribe, invaded Rome for decades and played a major role during the Empire's fall. They eventually split into western Goths (Ostrogoths) and eastern Goths (Visigoths). During the Middle Ages, a period from about 500 to 1500, a style of architecture called Gothic developed in Europe, but it had no direct relation to either tribe.

Gallienus may have given up some control over parts of the empire, but he strengthened his rule in the Roman lands he still governed. He brought better officers into the army, replacing senators who were often more concerned with personal and political gain than military discipline. Within the army, Gallienus developed a larger cavalry corps, to combat enemies who fought well on horseback. And his decision to let other leaders control parts of the empire let him focus on preserving order in the heart of Roman Europe.

After Gallienus, Aurelian (c. 215–275) was the most successful emperor during the period of anarchy. He came to power in 270 and began several military campaigns that restored imperial rule to Gaul and the eastern regions under Palmyran control. Fearing attacks on the city of Rome, Aurelian built a huge defensive wall. The emperor gave himself a new title: Restorer of the World. The problem of foreign invasion however, was not over. For the next 200 years, the empire continued its slow decline.

Diocletian's Reforms

In 284 Diocletian, a former commoner from Dalmatia, emerged as the next emperor. His reign marked the start of what some historians call the Dominate, which replaced the Principate founded by Augustus. Under the Principate, the emperors claimed to rule by the authority of the people and the Senate. Diocletian considered himself the *dominus*, the "lord and master" of Rome. The empire was now officially a dictatorship, with the emperor and the military in control. In practice, however, they had dominated since the late second century.

Although the emperor now claimed absolute power, Diocletian saw that he needed help running a struggling empire with many problems. He created a new form of leadership known today as the Tetrarchy. Diocletian had already chosen a co-emperor to rule in the west, while he ran the government in the east. Under the Tetrarchy, each of the co-emperors (known as Augustus) also had a "junior emperor" (called caesar) to help with military affairs. Each of these four rulers took control of a specific geographic region. Each had his own imperial court and could mint coins. All four put their names on laws and other imperial documents. Diocletian, however, was the ultimate ruler in the new arrangement.

Under the Tetrarchy, Rome strengthened its defenses and brought defeated invaders into its lands as citizens. During the 20 years Diocletian ruled, the government was stable. But after he and his co-emperor stepped down in 305, the transition to a new Tetrarchy was not smooth.

THE TETRARCHY

The name of Diocletian's government came from two Greek words adapted into Latin and then English: *tettares*, meaning "four," and *archos*, meaning "ruler." The word *tetrarchy* was first used in English around the 1630 to describe any government that featured four rulers sharing power. The two parts of that word also appear in other English words. Several mathematical and scientific terms have "tetra" at the beginning, noting four of something. A tetrad, for example is a group of four cells. The English version of *archos* is found in such words as *monarchy* and *oligarchy*—a government dominated by a small group of people who rule for their own benefit.

First Christian Emperor
Constantine is shown on this fourth century gold coin wearing a laurel wreath. Constantine was baptized a Christian shortly before his death.

The two junior emperors, Constantius (c. 250–306) and Galerius (d. 311), became senior emperors, and two new caesars joined the government. Constantius, based in Britain, died the next year, and his troops proclaimed his son Constantine the new Augustus in the west, even though he was not a caesar. Over the next two decades, Constantine waged several civil wars that eventually made him the sole ruler of the Roman Empire.

Constantine the Great

Constantine's key campaign came in 312, as he confronted forces led by Maxentius (d. 312), the son of another member of the first Tetrarchy. From his base in Gaul, Constantine marched on Rome. Before a major battle at the Milvian Bridge, Constantine supposedly received a heavenly sign indicating Jesus Christ and the Christian god were on his side. After his victory at the bridge, Constantine began to promote Christianity.

With imperial backing, Christians were soon free to worship openly, ending centuries of government restrictions on their faith. Along with his own personal belief in Christ, Constantine saw that this religion had social and political value. In his *History of Rome*, Michael Grant argues that the emperor and his aides believed the Christians "possessed universal aims and efficient, coherent organization that, in the long run, could unite the various conflicting peoples and classes of the empire in a single, all-embracing harmony." Shortly before his death in 337, Constantine was baptized, which made him an official member of the Christian Church. Because of Constantine's support of their religion, early Christian writers named him "the Great." In today's Greek Orthodox religion, this first Christian emperor of Rome is considered a saint.

With his victory over Maxentius, Constantine was the unchallenged ruler of the western half of the empire. The east was ruled by Licinius (c. 263–325), and in 316 the two rulers fought one another, with neither able to win a clear victory. They called a truce, but in 324 they battled again. This time Constantine defeated Licinius. For the first time in almost 100 years, Rome had a single, powerful emperor.

Constantine ruled the Roman Empire until his death in 337. He continued some of the reforms Diocletian had begun, such as trying to curb inflation and collect more taxes. In the military, he increased the number of Germans fighting for Rome in the provinces. Constantine also encouraged the idea of setting up imperial residencies throughout the empire. The members of the Tetrarchy lived in the regions they governed, since they could direct military operations more easily in the provinces than they could from Rome. Constantine also decided to build a new capital city in Byzantium, a Greek town on the Black Sea in what is now Turkey.

The "New Rome," as it was called, was renamed Constantinople. Its location, at a spot where Europe and Asia meet, made the new city a center for world trade. Like Rome, Constantinople was built on seven hills. Unlike the first capital, however, Constantine's new city had a deep natural harbor. In some ways, the emperor tried to recreate the old ways of Rome. The poor citizens received free grain, as earlier Romans had, and some senators move to Constantinople. Although the city of Rome remained important, imperial concerns began to focus more on the eastern half of the empire.

New Troubles

When Constantine died, his three stepsons took control of the government and split it into three parts. After years of fighting among the brothers, Constantius II (317–361) finally emerged as the sole leader in 353. Based in the west, he soon took on a co-emperor to rule in the east. His first choice was not reliable, however, so Constantius named one of his cousins, Julian (332–363). In 361, Julian became sole emperor, and although raised a Christian, he accepted pagan beliefs and tried to promote them throughout the empire.

CONNECTIONS >>>>>>>>>>>>>

The Council of Nicaea

Constantine took an active role in the Christian Church's early rules and beliefs. In 325, he summoned more than 300 bishops to the town of Nicaea, in what is now Turkey. Constantine wanted to end disagreements between the church leaders over official interpretations of the New Testament. He sided with the bishops who argued that God, Jesus Christ, and the Holy Spirit were three separate beings but each consisted equally of the same holy substance—forming a holy trinity. Other bishops, led by Arius, argued that Jesus was different from God and lesser than him in ultimate power. With Constantine's support, the first theory was accepted as the church's official belief, although for decades Arius and his supporters continued to challenge it. The creed, or statement of belief, that came out of the Nicaea conference is called the Nicene Creed. It remains at the heart of the teachings of the Roman Catholic Church and several other Christian churches.

THE ROMAN BUREAUCRACY

Just as they did in Rome, bureaucrats play an important role in keeping modern governments running smoothly. They are also sometimes called civil servants. The Roman government bureaucracy was based around departments, called *officia*, which led to such English words as *office* and *official*. The Roman bureaucrats collected taxes, ran government agencies, and kept the military well supplied. Just as today, Roman civil servants had specific rules for receiving promotions. Bureaucrats were also punished if they were caught accepting bribes. The Roman punishment, however, was a little harsher than today's fines or jail sentences: a bureaucrat found guilty had both hands cut off.

During this period the Romans continued to battle Germanic tribes along their northern borders. Julian also launched a large invasion of Persia, which ended with a Roman defeat and the emperor's death. The foreign battles continued for several decades, with major conflicts erupting against the Goths and native tribes of North Africa.

In one instance, however, the Goths actually sought protection from Rome against another tribe, the Huns. The emperor Valens (328–378) allowed the Goths to settle in Thrace, but the Romans treated the Goths badly, charging unfair prices for food or demanding humans as payment, so they could be sold as slaves. The Goths rebelled. In 378, at the Battle of Adrianople, more than 10,000 Romans, including Valens, died. The ancient historian Ammianus (c. 330–395) described the scene in his *History*, ". . .such great clouds of dust arose that it was hardly possible to see the sky. The air resounded with terrible cries. The darts, which brought death on every side, reached their mark and fell with deadly effect, for no one could see them quickly enough to place himself on guard. The barbarians, rushing on with their enormous army, beat down our horses and men and gave us no open spaces where we could fall back to operate."

The Romans kept the Goths from advancing to Constantinople, but the Goths continued to rampage in the Balkans. In 379, an Iberian general named Theodosius (c. 346–395) joined Gratian (359–383) as co-emperor. Theodosius ended the Gothic problem, forcing the Ostrogoths out of the Balkans and allowing the Visigoths to remain within the empire as allies. Theodosius also established Christianity as the one official state religion. Constantine and his successors had allowed pagan religions to exist side-by-side with Christianity. Theodosius closed pagan temples and ended rituals dedicated to the old gods.

Changes in Politics and Society

During the fourth century Rome struggled with ongoing wars, both civil and foreign, and a growing sense that the empire was two separate states. In the east the emperors tightened their control over the central government. They also spent money improving the military, which helped keep the region's economy strong. Cities and towns in the east generally did well, while many western cities experienced continued economic decline, a trend that had started in the third century. The increasing focus on the east meant less money was spent in the west, and the west faced greater military threats. In some cases, western city dwellers moved to the countryside to work on estates, which continued to grow in size.

Constantine's centralized government had created a growing number of bureaucrats—professional officials who worked in the government no matter who ruled the empire. The number of senators also grew, since Rome had a senate in both of its capital cities, and the western (Roman) senate expanded greatly throughout the century. In general, the empire's society began to separate into a small group of very wealthy people in the ruling class, and a growing number of poor workers.

The rise of the Christian Church gave its bishops growing influence over western Rome's politics and economy. Constantine allowed the churches to inherit property, and wealthy Christians donated land and money to their local churches. With the new wealth they controlled, bishops helped the poor and built churches, hospitals, and schools. They also had some power in non-religious affairs, because they could decide some legal disputes in their area.

A bishop could also use his religious role to influence the emperor. Ambrose (c. 340–397), the bishop of Milan, twice confronted Theodosius over civil issues. He convinced the emperor to rescind an order for Christians to rebuild a Jewish synagogue. The bishop also made Theodosius perform penance (prayers that ask for forgiveness) after Roman troops slaughtered residents of a Greek city.

Out With the Old Gods
Theodosius was the last emperor to reign over both the eastern and western halves of the empire. He established Christianity as the official state religion and closed the old Roman temples.

Changes in the West

With the death of Theodosius in 395, the empire once again split in two, this time for good. The trend of a strengthening eastern empire and declining western one continued. By now Milan, in the northern part of the Italian peninsula, served as the main home of the western emperor, since it was closer to the borderlands that faced frequent foreign attack. In the city of Rome and the surrounding countryside, the Senate regained its former role as the major political body. The senators, however, were generally more concerned with their personal wealth than with helping the emperors confront the forces that threatened the western empire's security.

By the fifth century, the most powerful of the German generals serving the empire were the true rulers in the west. None of them, however, claimed the title of emperor, knowing that the Romans would not accept a "foreigner" in that position. The Germans were content to select the emperors and influence their decisions. After Theodosius's death, the first influential German general in the west was Stilicho (c. 365–408) (he was actually half German and half Roman.) He hoped to reunite the eastern and western halves of the empire, with his sons eventually serving as emperors.

Theodosius had asked Stilicho to watch over his young son Honorius (384–423) until he was old enough to serve as emperor. In the east, another son of Theodosius, Arcadius (377–408), was emperor. He also had a military assistant, Rufinus (d. 395). As part of his plan to reunite the empire, Stilicho killed Rufinus. But before he could begin a direct military attack on the east, Stilicho had to combat Germanic tribes, first in the Alps, and then in the Italian peninsula. In 402, the Visigoth general Alaric (c. 370–410) led an invading force into the Italian peninsula. Stilicho drove off the Visigoths, but they returned the next year. In the heartland of the old Roman Empire, two German generals fought each other, using mostly German soldiers.

Years of Turmoil

In 406, various Germanic tribes crossed over the frozen Rhine River into Gaul. One of the major tribes was the Vandals, who eventually settled in the Iberian peninsula. The next year, the western empire lost control of Britain, as a commander named Constantine (d. 411) declared himself emperor (he was not related to Constantine the Great). He eventually took control of part of France and Spain, but was captured by Honorius's troops and executed.

In 408, Roman officials convinced Emperor Honorius that Stilicho was trying to harm the empire, and Honorius ordered his execution. At the time, Alaric was once again threatening the Italian peninsula. Honorius tried to work out a deal with the Visigoth ruler, just as Stilicho had before. The deals, however, never gave Alaric the power he wanted, and Rome lacked the military strength to stop him by force. In 410 Alaric's troops attacked Rome. They looted the city, but since the Visigoths were Christians, they did not destroy the churches. Alaric left Rome and hoped to conquer more of the Italian peninsula, but he died before completing his plan.

THE LATIN FATHERS

Ambrose was one of three important bishops from the Roman Empire who shaped the direction of the Christian Church in the west, leading to today's Roman Catholic Church. Ambrose, along with Augustine and Jerome (c. 340–420), are sometimes called the Latin Fathers, and all are considered saints. Jerome is famous for making the first Latin translation of the Bible from the original Greek and Aramaic (the Middle Eastern language Jesus spoke). Augustine was the major philosopher of the early western church. Ambrose, in addition to his confrontations with Theodosius, is known for a Latin saying that is still used today in English: "When in Rome, do as the Romans do." A fourth Latin Father, Pope Gregory I (c. 540–604), lived after the fall of the Roman Empire.

The Visigoths then invaded Gaul and Spain. Some of them set up their own state within southern Gaul. They had their own kings, but they agreed to provide military aide to the western empire. Another group of Visigoths founded a kingdom in Spain. Around this time, other tribes began to advance into the western empire, including the Franks and the Burgundians. Like the Visigoths in Gaul, these two peoples governed themselves, but offered help to Rome during wartime.

Imperial politics also threatened the western Empire during the first decades of the fifth century. For a time, various men were proclaimed emperor by the military or the invading Goths. The eastern empire also took part in the political battles in the west. During one crisis, Theodosius II (401–450), grandson of the great emperor, sent troops to the Italian peninsula to ensure that one of his relatives took the throne. His choice was Valentinian III (419–454), the eastern emperor's cousin. Valentinian was still a child, and another military man, Aetius (d. 454), actually controlled the western empire for many years.

The Huns

The Germanic tribes that invaded the Roman Empire were not simply looking to loot or weaken Roman power. They were facing their own military threat from an Asian people, the Huns, who had originally lived in Mongolia. Like other Mongolians, the Huns were nomadic–they moved frequently, seeking fresh pastures for their sheep and horses. In battle, they fought mostly on horseback and were known for their bravery and skill.

By the fifth century the Huns had reached the old Roman province of Dacia and territory that is now part of Hungary. In the east, Emperor

CONNECTIONS >>>>>>>>>>>>

The Vandals

Like several other Germanic tribes, the Vandals fought well against the Romans, but eventually they were defeated by a stronger military power. After spending about 20 years in Spain, the Vandals crossed the Mediterranean into North Africa, where they built a successful kingdom, taking control of the Roman provinces there. They built ships and carried out pirate raids in the western Mediterranean. The Vandal kingdom was finally destroyed around 523 by the Byzantine Empire. The Vandals' name lives on today in a region of southern Spain known as Andalusia (Al-Andalus is the Arabic name for "land of the Vandals), and in the English word *vandal*, a person who destroys other people's property for no reason.

Theodosius II paid them an annual tribute. In the west, the Huns tried to influence political affairs and sent troops to fight against the Theodosian Dynasty.

In 443 Attila (c. 406–453) killed his brother to take control of the Hun kingdom. Norman Cantor notes in his *Encyclopedia of the Middle Ages* that ancient historian Jordanes called Attila "a lover of war," although he could be fair to people who accepted his rule. Attila wanted to expand his kingdom westward into Europe. Certain leaders in Western Europe also thought Attila's potent army could help them achieve their own gains. Honoria (fifth century), the sister of Emperor Valentinian III, wanted the Huns to help her take control in the west, while the Vandals hoped for aid from the Huns against their enemies in Gaul.

Attila's horsemen headed for Gaul in 451, with the Vandals and Franks fighting as their allies. Near the city of Orleans, they fought a combined Roman and Visigoth force led by Aetius and Theoderic (d. 451), the Visigoth king. Neither side won a decisive victory. By some accounts, each army had more than 150,000 casualties.

Attila then turned south and rampaged through the Italian peninsula. His goal was to force Honoria to marry him, giving him control of part of the western Empire. In Rome, the Hun leader met with Pope Leo I (c. 390–461), who persuaded Attila to leave without taking his Roman bride. Disease within his ranks also convinced Attila to give up his march of conquest, and he died soon after. The kingdom he built collapsed soon after.

The End of the Western Empire

The invasions of the Italian peninsula did not end with Attila. In 455 the Vandals attacked Rome. For two weeks they stormed through the city, stealing almost anything they could carry. By this time the western half of the empire had shrunk considerably. The lands under central, imperial control were the Italian peninsula and parts of Gaul and Spain.

During the next 20 years, the west continued to face chaos. The events of the period, according to Allen Ward in *A History of the Roman People*, were "mind-numbingly complex." They involved Germans looking for power, competing Roman aristocrats, and the interests of the eastern emperor. Finally, in 476, German imperial troops in the Italian peninsula declared Odovacer (c. 434–493), a German chieftain, their king. That year is the date some historians use to mark the end of the old western empire and the rise of the separate Byzantine Empire in the east.

Although he had the support of his troops, Odovacer knew he needed political support as well. He refused the title of king and asked the eastern emperor, Zeno (c. 427–491), for his approval to rule in the west. Odovacer's successor, an Ostrogoth named Theoderic (c. 454–526), also ruled by the permission of the eastern empire, but the Italian peninsula was basically an independent Germanic kingdom. At the time, that situation was repeated across the west. The Franks ruled large parts of Gaul and western Germany, the Vandals had their kingdom in North Africa, the

CONNECTIONS >>>>>>>>>>>>>>>>>>>>>>>>>>>>>>>>

The Eastern Church

Constantinople was the main city of the eastern Christian Church, as well as the political capital of the Byzantine Empire. Four of the five main Christian bishops lived in eastern cities: Constantinople, Alexandria, Antioch, and Jerusalem. Only the bishop of Rome was not under the eastern emperor's political control. The emperors also tried to influence Church doctrine. Over time, the Roman bishop—the pope—developed an independence that led to conflicts with the eastern bishops. The eastern church was called orthodox, from two Greek words meaning "true belief." The

eastern emperor and his bishops thought their version of Christianity was the correct one.

The final split between the eastern and western churches came in 1054, officially creating the Roman Catholic Church in the west and the Orthodox Church in the east. By that time, Orthodox beliefs had spread into parts of Europe beyond the Byzantine Empire, particularly Russia. Today, Russia and large parts of Eastern and Southern Europe still practice Orthodox Christianity, and immigrants from those regions brought their faith to North America.

Justinian's Masterpiece
The dome and spires of Hagia Sophia still dominate the skyline of modern Istanbul.

Visigoths were in Spain, Angles and Saxons ruled much of Roman Britain, and the Burgundians controlled land along the Rhone River. As a political force, the Roman Empire in the west was dead.

The Eastern Empire

While the western half of the empire was crumbling, the eastern half remained strong. Today, the eastern empire is called the Byzantine Empire. The emperors there saw themselves as Roman, and Latin remained the chief language through the fifth century. Eventually, however, Greek became the official language. The emperors in Constantinople still considered the western lands part of their territory, at least in theory. In practice, however, they realized that the various Germanic kings in the region wielded local power and had only weak loyalties to the eastern empire.

Although the eastern empire was stronger than the west, it still faced outside threats from the Sassanids and the Huns. Unlike Rome, however, Constantinople was spared foreign invasion. The city was surrounded by water on three sides, and a huge wall protected it from a land invasion.

The east also had its own political intrigues, as German generals tried to gain influence the way they had in the west, and leaders sometimes struggled with bishops for power. One of the calmer periods came under Theodosius II, who ruled for almost 50 years (408–450). One of his greatest accomplishments was collecting all the laws passed since Constantine the Great and publishing them in one book, which is now known as the Theodosian Code.

After Theodosius II, another member of his family tried to preserve the dynasty founded by Theodosius the Great. His sister Pulcheria (399–453) influenced both the Church and government, with backing from a powerful German general. As a woman, she could not rule the empire, but she married Marcian (c. 396–457), a Roman who became emperor. The Theodosian Dynasty in the east ended with Pulcheria's death, and a new ruling family emerged starting with Leo I (c. 411–474, not the same as the pope of that name). With German backing, he was named emperor. His grandson and son-in-law followed him to the throne.

The last emperor with ties to Leo was Anastasius (491–518), who married Leo's daughter. Under him the empire continued to battle outsiders, including the Sassanids and a Central Asian tribe called the Bulgars. Anastasius helped strengthen the empire by reforming the tax laws. He ended some taxes and paid money from his own wealth to make up the difference in the state's funds. He also raised more money by ending corruption and making sure the taxes were properly collected. With his reforms, the Byzantine Empire expanded its economy and paid for its military needs.

The House of Justin

After Anastasius died in 518, he was replaced by one of his personal bodyguards, Justin (c. 450–527). Justin's nephew, Justinian I (c. 482–565), became emperor after him. Justinian's building projects and military conquests earned him the nickname "the Great." He also created a legal code that reviewed all existing Roman law, eliminating contradictions and making the legal system easier to understand. This Justinian Code formed the basis of law across Europe into modern times. (See chapter 4 for more information on the influence of Roman law.)

Justinian was driven to reunite the western and eastern halves of the empire. In 533 Byzantine troops conquered the Vandal kingdom of North Africa. Justinian then turned to the Italian peninsula and defeated the Ostrogoths. His gains in the west eventually included southern Spain (the Visigoth kingdom), part of southern France, and lands along the eastern shore of the Adriatic. Justinian took the title *autocrator*, or sole ruler of the world. Today, in English, an autocrat is someone who rules as an absolute dictator.

JUSTINIAN THE BUILDER

Along with his legal code, Justinian is best remembered today for his building projects in Constantinople. In 532, rioting in the city led to a great fire that destroyed public buildings and several churches. One of these, the Church of Holy Wisdom (Hagia Sophia in Greek), had been built by Constantine II (316–340) and rebuilt by Theodosius II. Justinian's Hagia Sophia featured a massive dome and was filled with marble, gold, and jewels. Centuries later, Muslim Turks took over Constantinople and turned the church into a mosque, an Islamic place of worship. Today Hagia Sophia is a church and a museum.

While winning these victories, however, Justinian left his empire open to attack in Asia Minor and the Middle East. He fought a long war with the Sassanids, and various barbarian tribes also battled his forces. In the end, the Byzantine Empire could not keep the territory it won in the west. Once again, barbarians reclaimed most of these lands, while Muslim Arabs eventually took North Africa and southern Spain.

Justinian's wars weakened the Byzantine Empire, leaving it open to invasion. The fighting also destroyed the imperial economy. Justinian also angered many of his subjects when he cracked down on people who did not accept his version of the Christian faith. A historian of his age, Procopius (c. 490/510–c. 560s), wrote in his *Secret History* that the emperor "encouraged civil strife and frontier warfare to confound the Romans, with only one thought in his mind, that the earth should run red with human blood and he might acquire more and more booty." Still, Justinian created a strong central state that survived for centuries, keeping the Greco-Roman culture alive in the east.

By the ninth century, the Byzantine Empire still controlled some parts of southern Italy. It also began to take back some of its former lands in the Middle East. The Byzantine influence also extended into what is now Russia, as the Slavic people of the region embraced the Eastern Orthodox religion. Until the early 11th century, the Byzantine Empire was the major political and military power in Europe and the Middle East. Then, Normans from France conquered parts of Italy and launched raids on Constantinople. From the west, a Turkish people known as the Seljuks also attacked.

Like the Roman Empire before it, the Byzantine Empire slowly began to decline. By the 14th century, its chief threat was a growing Islamic Empire in Asia Minor, ruled by the Ottoman Turks. Even with Slavic and Western European aid, the Byzantine emperors could not hold off the Turks. In 1453, the Ottoman Empire seized Constantinople. The old eastern Roman Empire was gone.

PART II

SOCIETY AND CULTURE

Politics and Society in the Empire

Living and Working in the Empire

Roman Art, Science, and Culture

CHAPTER 4

Politics and Society in the Empire

ALTHOUGH ANCIENT AND MODERN HISTORIANS DISAGREE over when Rome was founded, they do agree that the first rulers were kings. The first king probably appeared around the time the Forum was drained and paved with stone, around 625 B.C.E. The kings included several Etruscans, although Rome was not a colony of Etruria.

The role of the kings was also influenced by Etruscan political practices. As in Etruria, a king could not pass on his crown to a son or another relative. A new king had to win the approval of the leading men of the community, the *patres*. They looked for signs from the gods to show who should be the next king. The *patres*' choice then had to be approved by the *populus*—the Roman men who served as soldiers when the city faced attack. These men formed the Comitia Curiata, or Curiate Assembly. With the assembly's approval, the new king took his throne. Once a Roman king took power, he relied on the *patres* for advice. This group of advisors came to be called the Senate. Later, a new assembly, the Centuriate, replaced the Curiate Assembly, and other assemblies also developed over time.

Such English words as *populace, population,* and *popular* all come from the Latin word *populus*, the citizens who played the major role in Rome's political affairs. *Populus* also appears in an expression still widely used today: *vox populi*. The exact meaning of the phrase is "voice of the people." In a general sense, it means public opinion.

The Roman kings had many duties, including commanding the army, handling foreign affairs, and issuing laws designed to protect the city's security. The kings also served as the community's religious leader, the high priest. In Rome's political affairs, however, the kings sought

The Fasces

For the Etruscan kings, the fasces was a symbol of their power. The fasces was a bundle of rods surrounding a double-headed axe. It represented the kings' power to carry out the laws and punish criminals. The Romans also used the fasces as a symbol of government authority. When the Roman kingdom ended, the Senate continued to use the fasces to represent the power held by different elected officials, though the axe was removed while the magistrates were in Rome itself.

Fasces on a Roman church; an enduring symbol.

In the 20th century the fasces appeared again. In Italy Benito Mussolini (1883–1945) came to power in 1922. The name of his party was the Fascists, which came from the word fasces, and he used the Roman bundled rods and axe as a symbol of political power. Mussolini ruled as a dictator and hoped to build an overseas empire, just as Rome had done almost 2,000 years earlier. The word *fascist* came to mean anyone who supported a strong central government ruled by a single powerful leader. Fascists wanted close ties between the government and businesses, and supported using the military to expand their country's influence around the globe.

approval from the Curiate and Centuriate Assemblies for most of their actions. The monarchs also relied on the advice of senators, or elders of the community, whom they chose to help them govern. Throughout their history, the Romans did not have a written constitution. Instead, they relied on customs, tradition, and laws to define what their government was and how it operated.

The Family and Society

Rome first emerged as a state when families banded together to ensure everyone's survival against enemies and natural disasters. The interests of the various fathers in the community became the *res publica*, or "common concerns." The Latin word for country–*patria*–came from a word that means "belonging to the father." The English word *patriot* comes from this same Latin root.

Within the Roman family, the father held all the power. He was considered the owner of all the family's property, and even when his children reached adulthood he could direct their affairs. Fathers were also responsible for their children's education, and they might teach their children the basics of reading and writing. Later, during the Empire, most fathers sent their children to schools or hired tutors to teach them at home.

Dionysus of Halicarnassus (d. c. 7 B.C.E.), a Greek historian who lived in Rome during the first century B.C.E., wrote that the father's dominant role went back to the days of Romulus, the legendary founder of Rome (see page 15). According to the historian (as quoted in Jo-Ann Shelton's *As the Romans Did*), Romulus declared that the father "had absolute power over his son…whether he decided to imprison him, or whip him…or even kill him." Most fathers, however, did not take such extreme steps, and they were expected to consult with other adult family members when making decisions. But fathers did expect obedience from their children throughout their lives. And just as children were expected to respect and obey their fathers, citizens were supposed to show respect to the leaders of their community, who included men called fathers.

Fathers arranged marriages for their children, and important families might try to increase their wealth and power through these marriages. Roman families often included children from different parents. People did not live as long in Roman times as they do today (on average, a child who survived to age 5 could expect to live another 35 years), and when a husband or wife died, the remaining spouse often remarried, so having step-children or half-brothers or sisters was common.

A person who did not have an influential family might gain political, economic, or social support through a special relationship. Patrons were wealthy men who agreed to help less powerful men, called clients. The patron treated the client as if he were a member of his family, providing the same protection and help he would give his own children. (The Latin word for patron is related to *patres*, the word for father.) In return,

What's in a Name?

The importance of the family in ancient Rome appears in the names people used. As in today's world, Roman men had a first name and a last name. Later a third name was added. The first name was a personal name commonly used among family members. The second name, the *nomen*, corresponds to today's last name. For the Romans the *nomen* indicated a person's family or clan. The third name came after the *nomen* and was often a nickname based on a person's character, physical trait, or place of birth. This name, called the *cognomen*, could also be passed on from father to son. After the second century B.C.E., Roman names also included tribal names. Families or clans belonged to different tribes, which voted together in an assembly called the *comita tributa*.

The naming system was not the same for all Romans. In the earliest days women had only one name, a feminine version of their father's *nomen*. That meant sisters would have the same name. To avoid confusion, they were called "the elder" or "the younger." Toward the end of the Republic, women might also have a second name based on their father's *cognomen*. Slaves used only one name. If they won their freedom, they took the first name and family name of their former masters.

Roman Weddings

Unlike Westerners today, Romans did not need a church ceremony or approval from the state to marry. A marriage was a private agreement between the husband and wife and their families. But Romans did sometimes have celebrations that shared some features with today's weddings. One type of marriage ceremony featured eating a special cake, and marriages often took place in June, which is still a popular time for weddings in the United States. In one Roman custom, a bride was carried over a threshold—the floorboard at the bottom of a doorway—for good luck. Tripping over a threshold was considered bad luck. Today some grooms still follow this tradition and carry their brides over the threshold the first time they enter their new home as a married couple.

the client agreed to do what the patron asked and offer the same loyalty and obedience children owed their father. The patron was more powerful, yet legally he could not abuse that power to harm his client. According to the Twelve Tables, Rome's first set of written law, "Cursed be the patron who has done his client wrong" (quoted in Allen Ward's *A History of the Roman People*).

As the Roman Empire grew, the government used a similar patron-client system with some of its weaker neighbors, acting as their patron while these other countries were its clients. Rome would protect them from outside attack, and in return expected the client to provide money, natural resources, or military aid whenever Rome demanded it. It was better than being completely absorbed by the empire.

Slavery was also a part of Roman society, although the number of slaves was small during the earliest centuries. Slavery was considered a normal part of life throughout the Mediterranean world. After a military victory, the winners took some of the losing soldiers home with them as slaves. More than 100,000 people might be forced into slavery after a single Roman triumph. A person might also be ordered into slavery after committing a crime or failing to pay a debt. Pirates also raided ships and forced the passengers onboard into slavery. In some cases, poor parents sold their children into slavery. Slaves had no legal rights and could be sold whenever a slave owner chose.

During Rome's early years, slaves usually worked and lived with their owners on farms. Later, wealthy Romans used slaves to run their households and operate small businesses. Local governments also used slave labor to build roads and public buildings. Many owners eventually freed their slaves.

The Birth of the Republic

Roman historians wrote that during the sixth century B.C.E., their kings began to rule as tyrants. Livy suggests that an Etruscan named Tarquin the Proud (r. 534–509 B.C.E.) was the worst of these dictators, and that in 509 the Roman people rebelled against him. Modern historians do not completely accept Livy's story. Some believe he simplified how the monarchy ended and that Rome saw a series of conflicts within the ruling class. Still, modern historians do agree that the monarchy ended around that time. In its place, the Romans created the Republic.

The *patres* seemed to play the biggest role in creating the new Roman government. Their goal was to prevent the rise of new tyrants who would take away their traditional rights. The *patres* formed the heart of the patrician class, which dominated Roman society.

Instead of choosing a new king, the *patres* elected two officials, called consuls. Each consul could serve for just one year, and each held *imperium* (military and political power) and eventually commanded his

In the Senate
The idea of Rome's representative government has been a powerful symbol throughout history. This painting by Cesare Maccari (1840–1919) adorns the wall of the Palazzo Madama in Rome. It shows Cicero (see page 99) speaking before the Senate.

own legion. The consuls served as judges and could propose laws for the Centuriate Assembly to consider. They could also veto one another's decisions. Consuls and other public officials were all called magistrates, a term still used to describe some government officials. The Senate remained as a group of advisors for the consuls. As before, Rome's wealthiest and most powerful citizens served as senators. The Centuriate Assembly played a key role in the new government, electing most top government officials.

By the fifth century B.C.E., Rome's plebs began to demand a say in the new government. Some plebs had built large fortunes, and a few were elected to the consulship. Over time, however, the patricians pushed them out of powerful positions. Poorer plebs could not serve in the hoplite or other branches of the military that carried the most social status. The plebs, rich and poor, wanted their own power in the Republican government. In 494 B.C.E. the plebs formed an assembly and elected their own magistrates, called tribunes. Their goal was to protect the plebs from unfair laws. Anyone who physically hurt tribunes or tried to limit their actions was breaking a religious law that protected them from harm. A tribune's attacker could be killed without penalty.

Over time the plebs elected other officials and began to play a larger role in the Republic. The plebs formed a tribal council that voted on different proposals concerning economic and military affairs. Their vote was called a *plebiscita*. In English the word *plebiscite* is still used today to describe a vote among all citizens on important issues. The patricians did not have to accept the results of a plebiscite, but the vote often influenced their decisions.

In 367 B.C.E. the plebs won a major political victory when they were officially allowed to hold the office of consul. Only the wealthiest plebs, however, could afford to hold the position, which was unpaid. Rome's ruling class, which had once been dominated by the patricians, now included wealthy *equites* and plebs. The plebs also eventually won the right to hold religious offices, which the patricians had previously dominated.

By the late third century B.C.E., Roman politics and society was completely controlled by the city's wealthiest families. Romans accepted the idea that some people were naturally better than others, and that everyone in society held a specific rank. In general, people of lower ranks did not challenge the people above them. The upper classes, on the whole, did not care about the lives of the poorer people beneath them.

THE TWELVE TABLES

Around 450 B.C.E., the plebs' growing power forced the patricians to meet their demand to write down Roman laws for the first time. Before this, patrician priests kept track of the laws and decided what they meant. The laws were written down on 12 pieces of bronze and were known as the Twelve Tables. All Romans could now find out exactly what the laws were and their rights under them. The laws dealt with civil issues—the duties of citizens to the state and the relations between citizens. The Twelve Tables, however, did not introduce any new laws that granted the plebs new rights or powers, as they had wanted.

Roman Law

One of Rome's most important political and social developments was its highly structured legal system. As in the U.S. legal system today, Rome had two major classes of laws: civil and public (today called criminal law). Civil laws dealt with such things as business and property, while public law focused on crimes, such as murder, theft, and assault. Laws regarding religion were also considered public. The Roman court system had religious roots. In the early days of the Republic, religious advisors called pontiffs interpreted the laws, both civil and public. The pontiffs were not lawyers or judges, but their decisions affected how the laws were applied.

Cicero (106–43 B.C.E.), a Roman politician and scholar, noted the importance of law to the Ro-

---

CONNECTIONS >>>>>>>>>>>>

Legal Language

The Latin word for law is *lex* (the plural is *leges*). That word led to many English words related to laws. Legislators are the elected officials who make laws, and the word *legal* also comes from *leges*. The words *judge* and *judicial* also have Latin roots.

Many legal terms are Latin, since European scholars used Latin for many years. In fact, law schools in some European nations still require their students to study Latin. English settlers brought this language to North America, and it is still used in courts today. Some of the more common phrases include *habeas corpus* and *amicus curiae*. Habeas corpus means "you have the body" and refers to a legal procedure that forces the state to prove it has enough evidence to hold someone it has arrested. Amicus curiae, or "friend of the court," is a person or group that has an interest in a particular court case and presents pertinent information to the court.

---

mans. As quoted by Jo-Ann Shelton in *As the Romans Did*, Cicero wrote that "equality under the law [was] a right which free people cherish." Throughout the history of the Republic, the Centuriate Assembly made most decisions of central, political importance, including passing laws. In moments of crisis, some politicians made use of the legislative power of the plebs and their plebiscites. Under the emperors, the role of the people in both elections and lawmaking declined considerably, while the power of the Senate was, for a time, enhanced.

Roman citizens could not go to a government office or the police and have someone arrested. People who believed they had been wronged had to begin legal actions on their own. The winner of a court case also had to act on his own to enforce whatever punishment was handed out, except in cases that involved the execution of a convicted person. At trials, magistrates served as judges and some of their verdicts could be appealed to the assemblies. Several well-educated Romans tried to help

CONNECTIONS >>>>>>>>>>>>>>>>>>>>>>>>>>>>>>>>>>>>

The Roman Senate and the U.S. Senate

Although the Roman Senate and the U.S. Senate share the same name, they have many differences. By the late Republic, any Roman elected to serve as a magistrate automatically was part of the Senate, and senators served for life. All Roman senators (and magistrates) were men. U.S. senators can be either men or women, and they are elected to terms that last six years, although they can run for reelection as often as they like. The Roman Senate did not pass laws, though it could issue decrees, which shaped the actions magistrates took. In the United States the Senate is a vital part of the legislative process.

The size of the two senates also varied. Voters in each U.S. state elect two senators; the current membership is 100. At its founding, the Roman Senate had 100 members, but the number reached 1,000 by the time Augustus came to power. He cut back the Senate to 600 and required senators to have a certain amount of property before they could serve. U.S. senators do not have to meet any financial requirements, although the Senate has sometimes been called "the Millionaires' Club," because it tends to attract many wealthy people who have the large sums of money required to run for office.

The two bodies have one shared trait: Some of Rome's best orators (public speakers) were its senators, who often gave long, emotional speeches on public issues. The U.S. Senate is considered a source for some of America's best public speakers, as well, and the Senate allows one speaker to talk for hours at a time.

Look at the painting on page 67 to see how similar the layout of our United States Senate chamber is to the ancient Roman Senate.

other citizens in the courts by offering legal aid. Using different legal handbooks, a person pursuing a court case did not have to rely on the pontiffs.

During the second century B.C.E., Rome set up its first permanent criminal courts. These dealt with major crimes, and senators sat on the juries to decide a person's innocence or guilt. These courts lasted into the imperial era, when the Senate began to hear most criminal cases. The emperor could also hear some cases. In the empire's provinces, governors served as judges, hearing criminal cases throughout the region. Local courts heard civil matters, but Roman citizens could not be tried in these provincial courts. In court, Roman citizens under the empire were eventually divided into two separate classes, and the wealthy and powerful received lighter punishments than the common people.

Troubles in a Changing Society

Rome's expansion in the Italian peninsula and then overseas led to some changes in its political and social life at home. The Senate began to play a larger role in running the government. Although only the assemblies could pass laws, the Senate could propose them, and it also issued decrees. Magistrates usually carried out the Senate's decrees.

As the Senate gained power, its members also sought personal wealth. After 218 B.C.E. senators could not engage in commerce, so many focused on buying land and creating huge farms, called *latifundia*. The senators built these estates at the expense of farmers with small plots of land. Many of these farmers had to serve in the military, preventing them from running their farms efficiently. If a soldier-farmer died in combat, his family often had trouble working the land, so poor, struggling farm families often sold out to the wealthy. In his work *Civil Wars*, the ancient historian Appian (d. c. 160) noted that many typical Italians were "hard pressed by poverty, taxes, and military service" (as quoted in Jo-Ann Shelton's *As the Romans Did*).

By the middle of the second century B.C.E., Rome had a growing number of landless peasants. Since military service was based on wealth, the Republic found that it had a shrinking supply of army recruits. In 133 B.C.E., a tribune named Tiberius Gracchus (c. 164–133 B.C.E.) proposed a solution. He wanted to break apart large holdings of public land and give the land to the peasants. According to the Roman historian Plutarch, writing in his *Lives of the Noble Grecians and Romans*, Tiberius said the Republic's soldiers, "having no houses or settlements of their own, are

July and the Julian Calendar

One honor the Senate gave Julius Caesar was renaming the month of his birth for him. What had been called Quintilius, Latin for "fifth month," became Julius. The modern English July comes from that name. Caesar also created a calendar called the Julian calendar. This replaced the old Roman calendar that had 355 days and began on March 1. Using the Egyptian calendar as a model, Caesar made the year 365 and a half days long, starting on January 1. That calendar is still used throughout the Western world, although in 1582 Pope Gregory XIII (1502–1585), the head of the Roman Catholic Church at the time, made some minor changes to it. This modified Julian calendar is called the Gregorian calendar.

constrained to wander from place to place with their wives and children."

The land reform law passed despite opposition from the Senate. Tiberius Gracchus had angered the senators when he did not consult with them before proposing his reform. He also came into conflict with the other tribune of the plebs at the time when Tiberius called for a vote to have his rival removed from office—something the Romans had never done before.

Eager to pursue his reform, Tiberius decided to run for a second term as tribune. This step was not illegal, but highly unusual, and it led to further grumbling from his critics. A group of senators accused him of trying to rule as a tyrant, and they organized a mob that attacked Tiberius and his supporters. About 300 people—including Tiberius Gracchus—died in the rioting.

Within a decade, Tiberius's brother, Gaius Gracchus (d. 121 B.C.E.), became a tribune, and he wanted to extend his brother's reforms. Gaius also hoped to gain some revenge for his brother's murder and increase his own political power. To help the farmers, he built roads that connected the countryside with city markets. To feed the poor, he passed the Grain Law, under which the Roman government bought wheat overseas and sold it in Rome at a fixed price, which kept the price of wheat affordable. In general, Gaius's actions won him support among the *equites* and the poor, while angering many of the senators. They saw the changes as a threat to their power and wealth. Gaius, like his brother, died when his opponents in the Senate attacked him and his supporters.

The actions of the Gracchus brothers (known collectively as the Gracchi) led to the creation of two distinct political groups: the *optimates* and the *populares*. The *optimates*, or "best men," wanted to preserve the Senate's power and favored using force to end any public emergencies. The *populares* claimed to represent the general population and would take action without the Senate's approval. In general, however, the leaders of both groups came from the same wealthy class of Romans. Their political conflicts were often based on personal hatreds and a hunger for power, not a desire to carry out a political philosophy.

Difficult Years

During the civil war years of the first century B.C.E., a new type of government emerged in Rome. The generals Pompey, Crassus, and Julius Caesar united to take on their critics in the Senate. They formed a triumvirate, a government that shares power among three leaders.

The three leaders had an uneasy relationship. Crassus and Pompey had been rivals before. Caesar, though not as well known as a general, was eager to gain power and prestige. As consul, Caesar pressed the passage of laws that helped him build his wealth and his military forces. He eventually emerged as Rome's supreme leader, paving the way for the first emperor.

Although many Romans at first welcomed Julius Caesar as a hero, restoring order in a time of chaos, he had enemies in the Senate. These senators believed Caesar was a threat to the republican system and their own influence in Roman society. They feared Caesar was trying to bring back the monarchy. In February 44 B.C.E., Caesar used his growing power to have himself named dictator for life. He also placed statues of himself around Rome and accepted special honors that placed him above any other magistrate, such as his own gold-covered throne.

Politics and Society in Imperial Rome

With Caesar's assassination, another civil war broke out, leading to a second triumvirate, created in 43 B.C.E., consisting of Marc Antony, Octavian, and Lepidus. This triumvirate had legal limits on its role and how long it would last, and was followed by the rule of the first emperor, Octavian, who took the title Augustus. At various times under Augustus and future emperors, the Senate tried to regain some of its old influence. In general, however, the emperors were able to control more of the government. They appointed officials who played a larger role in directing the state's affairs, at the expense of elected magistrates and the assemblies.

For women, a trend that had started during the last two centuries of the Republic continued under the empire. Among the patricians, women played a larger role in family matters and political affairs as they gained

---

INFLUENTIAL WOMEN

Most of the famous women of ancient Rome were connected to the important political families of the late Republic and the empire. Some of these leading ladies included Cornelia (second century B.C.E.), daughter of the famous general Scipio Africanus and mother of the political reformers the Gracchi; Livia (58 B.C.E.–29 C.E.), wife of Augustus; and Agrippina the Younger (15–59), wife of Claudius and mother of Nero. Julia Domna (c. 167–217), wife of the emperor Septimius Severus, was perhaps the most honored woman during the Roman Empire. She received the title "Mother of the Fatherland," and statues of her were erected around Rome. During the third century, she and her sister, Julia Maesa, and her niece, Julia Mamaea, played a large role in running imperial affairs.

their own sources of income. Wealthy soldiers who died in battle left their fortunes to their wives. A woman who remarried then had control over that money, because changes in marriage laws meant that males in her own family, not her husband, controlled her actions. Since a wealthy woman's male relatives were usually not living in her house and may not have been in the same town, the woman had greater freedom over her money and her life.

Wealthy families in the empire also made more of an effort to educate their daughters than in the past. This greater learning helped give women more influence in society, at least in personal affairs—women still could not take part in politics. However, the growing influence of women did not reach into the lower classes of Rome. In 90, the historian Plutarch held a still-common view about wives and women in general. In his work *Moral Advice* he said, "A wife should have no emotion of her own, but share in the seriousness and playfulness...of her husband" (as quoted in Jo-Ann Shelton's *As the Romans Did*).

In general, the wealthy could afford better education for their children—both boys and girls—than could the poor. Still, the Romans valued learning, and most people during the empire period knew the basics of reading and writing. Poor students might learn some basics at home or with a local tutor, but their schooling ended by the time they were 10 or 11 years old. Children from wealthier families, usually boys, went on to a teacher called a *grammaticus*. (This Latin word means "from letters" and is the root source of the English word *grammar*.) With a *grammaticus*, students improved their reading and writing skills

Household Slaves
This ancient relief carving shows slaves at work in the kitchen of a wealthy Roman home.

and learned Greek. A small number of teenage boys received further private education to prepare them for certain careers, such as law or politics.

During the empire, the wealthy—patricians, plebs, and *equites*—still dominated the economy and society, even if they lost political power to the emperor and his advisors. The poor, however, faced even harder times, especially if they lived outside Rome or important provincial cities. In those places the emperors tried to provide aid, but in most parts of the empire the poor struggled to live. The middle classes—merchants and farmers without big estates—also had trouble coping as taxes rose over time.

Conditions for slaves had been improving since the late Republic. Still, at times slaves used

Spartacus and the Slave Rebellion

During the later years of the Republic, Rome put down several slave revolts. The largest and longest revolt started in 73 B.C.E., led by Spartacus. A slave from Thrace, Spartacus was trained to fight as a gladiator. He battled other gladiators and wild animals in games held to amuse the Romans. Spartacus organized other slaves, who broke away from their masters and stole weapons for the revolt. Spartacus eventually assembled a slave army of about 70,000 soldiers and terrorized the Italian countryside. Along the way he defeated several Roman armies. Government forces finally defeated Spartacus in 71 B.C.E., killing him and slaughtering thousands of his troops.

The story of Spartacus was made into an award-winning film in 1960. In 2004, a remake of *Spartacus* appeared on television.

force to challenge their owners and the limitations placed on them. Large numbers of slaves often worked together on the *latifundia*. The slaves outnumbered their masters and could join forces in a revolt. After the rebellion (see the box above) led by Spartacus (d. 71 B.C.E.), some slave owners tried to treat their slaves more fairly. Slaves with training and education—doctors, cooks, teachers—certainly lived better lives. Historian Allen Ward writes in *A History of the Roman People* that slaves "in the service of wealthy and powerful masters often fared better than the majority of free citizens."

A growing number of masters freed their slaves. These freedmen, as they were called, often went on to become successful business owners and had a patron-client relationship with their old masters. Some slave owners granted slaves their freedom in a formal legal ceremony. In that case, the freedmen became Roman citizens. These freedmen could not run for political office, but their children could.

Rome and Its Provinces

Roman society always included more than the people born in Rome and the immediate surroundings. From its earliest days, Rome had important contact with other peoples, particularly the Etruscans and Greeks. According to one legend, Romulus invited all the exiles on the Italian peninsula to come to his city. In the beginning, Rome had just three tribes that voted on laws and defended the city. By the late Republic, it had 35 tribes, as people from other towns were granted Roman citizenship. That trend of bringing outside people into the government and society continued during the empire.

Gaining Roman citizenship was important for non-Romans. As citizens, they could take part in politics and receive certain legal protections. The Romans first gave citizenship to their Latin allies, then eventually spread the privilege throughout the Italian peninsula—but only after the Social War (see page 26). Julius Caesar granted citizenship to the people in some colonies he founded, and both he and Marius before him granted citizenship to the soldiers they recruited in southern Gaul. To these men, the benefits of becoming citizens were worth the risk of dying in battle.

As the Roman Empire grew, the emperors also gave more rights and privileges to people from the provinces. Vespasian, who ruled from 69 to 79, was one of the first emperors to do this, bringing more provincials into the Senate and other parts of the government. Later, Septimius did the same, along with naming more *equites* to the Senate.

In general, these changes gave emperors a new group of loyal supporters in Rome, while weakening the influence of the city's local patrician families. The last major policy on citizenship came in 212,

Foreigners and Barbarians

To the ancient Greeks, anyone who was not Greek was called a *barbaros*—a foreigner. The word, however, also had a stronger, negative meaning, suggesting that the foreigner was ignorant because he did not speak or understand the Greek language. The Romans did not look down so harshly on foreigners, although they adapted the Greek word *barbaros* to the Latin *barbarus*, which had roughly the same meaning.

The English word *barbarian* comes from these ancient words; it means someone who is crude and uncivilized. A barbarian might also commit a barbarity, or cruel and violent act. Past historians often referred to the various tribes that invaded the Roman Empire as barbarians, reflecting Rome's attitude toward people it considered inferior. In reality, however, many of these tribes had already adapted Roman ways or developed their own worthwhile cultures.

when the emperor Caracalla granted citizenship to all free men throughout the empire.

Even before granting citizenship to all the provincials, Rome heavily influenced life in the lands it conquered. The process of making the provinces more like Rome is known today as Romanization. Julius Caesar started this process by building Roman schools in the western part of the empire. They taught the basics of reading, writing, and arithmetic to young children. Roman citizens settled in the provinces, bringing their language and customs, and Roman officials carried out policies that were in the government's interests. Emperors built temples to the Roman gods and public buildings similar to the ones in the capital city. Before gaining Roman citizenship, some provincials received Latin rights. Although one step below full citizenship, these rights made residents more loyal to Rome, and the most ambitious provincials won jobs in the Roman government. Latin rights gave the provincials legal protection in business dealings and trials. The growing role of provincials in the army and government eventually led to the first non-Roman emperors.

Through the centuries, the people conquered by Rome also influenced the Romans. The Greeks had the greatest influence, and the link between ancient Greece and Rome is seen today in the idea of a Greco-Roman heritage that shaped the Western world. In the eastern half of the empire, Greek was one of the official languages. In Rome, scholars looked to Greece for ideas about art, philosophy, and government. The Romans respected the learning and intelligence of the Greeks and often hired them as teachers and doctors. The Romans also brought many Greek words into the Latin language. Paradoxically, the Romans also generally had a low opinion of the Greek character, often accusing Greeks of being deceitful and having low morals.

CHAPTER 5

Living and Working in the Empire

OVER THE CENTURIES, ROME GREW FROM A GROUP OF small villages into a capital city of more than 1 million people. The city offered many economic opportunities, as did government service throughout the empire. Two occupations, however, dominated Roman society throughout much of its history: farming and military service. The Romans cherished the values associated with a successful farmer and a courageous soldier. They saw such traits as hard work and determination leading to great accomplishments in both fields. Even if individuals made their fortune and pursued a life of leisure, in theory the Romans still believed most people should live like the sturdy farmers and soldiers that built the Republic and the empire. The poet Horace (65–8 B.C.E.) wrote in *The Pleasures of Country Life*, "Happy is the man who, far removed from business . . . cultivates his ancestral farm with his oxen, free from all interest."

Life on the Farm

In Rome's early days, most citizens owned their small farms. Over time, however, the vast number of free farmers worked as tenants for large landowners. They paid the owners rent and kept the crops they raised. Some landowners also used a system called sharecropping: Instead of charging rent, they took a share of the crops their tenants raised. Slaves were also used to work large farms, although the number of slaves on farms began to decrease during the first century B.C.E. Owning and taking care of slaves was more expensive than simply hiring tenant farmers.

From the end of the Republic on, most tenants and farmers who owned their own small plots of land struggled to survive. Farm life was difficult, centering on a long list of never-ending chores. Farmers and their

OPPOSITE
Protective Headgear
This first-century B.C.E. Roman bronze helmet shows scenes of a city being sacked.

CONNECTIONS >>>>>>>>>>>>

Close to the Soil

The Romantic idea that farmers lived better lives and made better citizens then city residents continued well past the end of the Roman Empire. In the United States, President Thomas Jefferson often wrote that farmers' values and their close ties to the land made them the best citizens. He proposed policies meant to help protect the farmers' interests over the economic concerns of merchants and bankers. That notion also shaped the political policies of President Andrew Jackson and U.S. politicians known as populists—a word related to the Latin word *populares*, the Roman political faction that supported the common people.

families typically raised grain, vegetables, fruit, and livestock. They also harvested grapes and olives, which they sold to the larger estates.

For the poor and most workers, wheat was a main part of their diet, either as bread or made into a porridge called *puls*. Most families did not have their own ovens for baking bread, although large farms did have them. Meat was rarely served in a poor Roman's home. More common were beans and local fruit. Wine or vinegar mixed with water was a common drink.

In the provinces, the average people faced some of the same difficulties the typical Roman farmer faced. In addition, the provincials dealt with the extra demands Rome placed on them in the form of taxes and tribute—money or goods that ensured Rome would not attack them. The provincials had to provide food—and sometimes shelter—for the soldiers, in addition to the products they sent to Rome. The Romans argued that even if the provincials suffered some difficulties, they received something better in return: The Pax Romana protected them from outside attack and created an economic system that eventually brought new wealth to the provinces. In general, these claims were correct. The Romans brought order and prosperity to many of their provinces.

Military Life

During Rome's early years, farmers formed the backbone of its military. Only landowners fought; Rome's leaders assumed that people defending their own and their neighbors' farms would fight harder than someone who had no ties to the land. In the time of the general Marius, however, during the first century B.C.E., Rome began to develop its first professional army. Becoming a soldier was a promising—if risky—career for poor farmers or others who could not find work. At first, most soldiers came from the Italian peninsula, but as the empire grew, citizens from all over joined the ranks.

Marius recruited soldiers by giving them weapons and equipment. Before this, Roman soldiers were required to provide their own weapons. Soldiers signed up for 16 years, a term later extended to 20. These career soldiers were called legionnaires, while their officers were called centurions. After completing their service, the legionnaires were on reserve for another five years, meaning they could be called back to duty during an emergency.

Roman soldiers carried deadly weapons. A legionnaire was equipped with a dagger called a *pugio*, a short iron sword called a *gladius*, which was used for stabbing and slashing, and a javelin called a *pilum*. By about 35 C.E., Roman soldiers wore armor made of sections of iron joined by hooks or leather straps. They carried shields made of layers of wood glued together and covered in leather and linen. Bronze and iron helmets were designed to protect the sides of the head and neck. Officers wore crests on their helmets so they could be easily seen during a battle.

Soldiers received a salary from the generals who commanded them or from the emperor, as well as occasional bonuses—the booty they took from their defeated enemies. Augustus offered a special bonus to legionnaires who completed their entire term of service—money equal to more than 13 years' pay. Some soldiers, once they retired, had enough money to open businesses and move up into the *equites* class.

Rome's army was famous for its discipline and skill. Flavius Joseph, a Jewish historian of the first century, wrote about Roman soldiers in *A History of the Jewish War*, "As if born for the sole purpose of wielding arms, they never take a break from training, never wait for a situation requiring arms" (as quoted in Jo-Ann Shelton's *As the Romans Did*). New recruits went on 20-mile marches three times a month, with their supplies and weapons on their backs, to prepare them for battle. Legionnaires who disobeyed their officers were executed—even if their actions led to success on the battlefield.

To keep the legionnaires focused on their military activities, Augustus said they could not marry, though many men had relationships with women and had children.

The military also offered good opportunities to provincials. Only Roman citizens could be legionnaires, but the men of the provinces were recruited as auxiliaries. They usually served under Roman officers. Auxiliaries received less pay than the regular troops and had to serve 25 years, but if they completed their service they and their families were granted Roman citizenship.

ENFORCING MILITARY DISCIPLINE

In English, to *decimate* something means to destroy it completely. The word comes from the Latin *decimare*, which means to kill every 10th person. If a group of Roman soldiers tried to mutiny, their officer would randomly take one soldier out of every 10 and kill him. This decimation served as a warning to other soldiers who might consider rebelling. Roman troops would also sometimes decimate captured enemy soldiers. The root of *decimare* is the Latin word for 10, which also appears in such English words as *decimal* and *decade*.

Roman Fashion

Romans of all classes wore similar clothing, with some important differences. The most common item was the tunic, a long shirt with short sleeves. Romans usually tied a belt around the waist of the tunic. In public, male citizens often wore a toga over the tunic. This wool garment was draped over one shoulder and reached to the floor.

Certain government officials and senators wore togas with purple stripes. The emperor's toga was completely purple. Because purple dye was expensive, the color purple was often associated with royalty and the wealthy. Black togas were worn at funerals, and men running for office wore togas rubbed with chalk, which made them especially white.

Women also wore tunics. Married women wore a *stoa* over their tunics for modesty. This article of clothing was similar to a long dress. Soldiers often wore short leather trousers. Some people, both men and women, wore capes made of wool or leather. Some capes had hoods. In general, children wore smaller versions of the clothes their parents wore.

Crafts and Trade

Rome's growth from a small farming community to the largest city in the world created job opportunities for many people. From its earliest days, Romans had a product they could trade with other peoples: salt. Romans collected it along the mouth of the Tiber River. Salt not only added flavor to foods but also helped preserve them. Another important early product was wine. During the sixth century B.C.E., the Romans sold wine to the Carthaginians as well as their closer neighbors in the Italian peninsula.

Trading with their neighbors, the Greeks and the Etruscans, Romans had access to goods from a wide geographic area. Ivory came from the Middle East or Africa, while amber came from northern Europe. Roman artisans learned to make beautiful and practical items out of imported materials such as these, as well as local resources and metals. By the time of the Republic, Rome was trading handcrafted goods around the Mediterranean, especially pottery and bronze items. In return, Rome received the grain and other foods it needed to feed its growing population.

As Rome's empire expanded beyond the Italian peninsula, it traded with more distant lands. Roman glassware has been found in what is now Norway and southern Russia, and metal goods also reached a wide market. After Augustus, trade with Asia increased. Romans wanted luxury items from the East—silk from China, spices from India and nearby islands. Other popular imported goods included perfumes and gems. The

THE SPICE TRADE

The word *spice* comes from the Latin *species*, meaning outward appearance or form. In English, the related word *specie* refers to payment with coins. Romans cherished spices from Asia because they were so rare and added interesting tastes to their meals. Only the wealthy could afford spices, and Romans could not produce the Eastern spices themselves, since the plants they came from could only grow in certain climates. The prized spices included pepper, ginger, and nutmeg.

Romans paid for these items with gold and silver, since they did not have comparable luxury goods to trade in return.

During the second century, the Greek writer Aristides (118–c. 180) described Rome's trading activity. In his work *To Rome* (as cited by Colin Wells in *The Roman Empire*), Aristides wrote, "Whatever each people raises or manufactures is undoubtedly always here to overflowing . . . the city seems like the common warehouse of the world." Soon after Roman troops won a victory, traders followed, setting up businesses to export needed items to Rome. Some of these traders worked for themselves, while others worked for large companies. The traders used the Roman road system built for moving soldiers to transport their goods. Items from more distant lands came by ship. Rome lacked its own port, but in the first century Claudius built Portus–"the Harbor"–near the older port town of Ostia, about 18 miles from Rome. The English word *port* comes from this Roman port city.

One Style Fits All
Augustus's family all wore tunics with togas over them–as did most Romans. Children just wore smaller versions of their parents' clothes.

Rome also traded with parts of Africa beyond the empire's borders. Some of the most prized goods from that region were exotic animals that did not live in Europe. Some, such as parrots and monkeys, were kept as pets by the rich. Other animals, such as crocodiles, lions, leopards, and elephants, were used in the gladiatorial games held in Rome and other cities. The animals fought each other to the death, as well as fighting gladiators. During one game the emperor Commodus killed five hippopotami. The Roman government spent large amounts of money to capture, transport, and take care of all these foreign beasts, a sign of the empire's wealth–and its tendency to waste it.

City Work

The city of Rome was the economic heart of the empire. Its growth offered opportunities to people with skill or money to invest in a small business. Similar opportunities developed in smaller cities around the empire,

A Taste of Rome

Today at Porta Maggiore, one of the surviving city gates of ancient Rome, stands the tomb of Eurysaces, a wealthy baker who died in 30 B.C.E. The tomb is shaped like an oven, and a relief carving shows Eurysaces and his slaves pulling a loaf of bread from the oven—a round loaf called *ciambella* that is still widely eaten in Europe today. Many other ancient Roman cooking techniques, flavors, and ingredients also turn up in modern Italian cooking. For example, the ancient Romans enjoyed flatbreads, sometimes topped with vegetables or cheese—ancient pizza. The Romans used a cooking condiment called *garum*, made from fermented anchovies and sea salt, that is much like the salted anchovies and anchovy paste used today in Italian cooking. The peasants thickened their soup with dried bits of dough—just as modern Romans toss dried pasta into a pot of soup. *De agricultura*, a book about agriculture and food written by Roman statesman Cato (234–149 B.C.E.) and published in about 180 B.C.E., gives the very first published recipe for a layer cake.

with some provincial cities becoming centers of a particular trade. Capua, in Italy, for example, was known for all kinds of silver ware, while Patavium (the modern Italian city of Padua) was famous for wool clothing. Lugdunum (Lyons, France) was a glassmaking center, and cities in Asia Minor produced such goods as carpets and cloth.

A typical city in Roman times had many of the same businesses and professions that thrive in modern cities. Pompeii, which was destroyed by the eruption of Mount Vesuvius in 79, offers a good example. Although small compared to Rome, the city had all the merchants and shops urban Romans needed to live their daily lives: barbers, surgeons, bakers, cloth makers, carpenters, goldsmiths, and grocers. Some professions in Pompeii not usually seen today included mule driving and mat making. Less educated or skilled people could find short-term jobs, such as unloading ships or doing errands for the wealthy.

Two types of business provided many job opportunities in Rome and throughout the empire: construction and finance. The various emperors' building projects created jobs for laborers and people who manufactured and transported building materials. The Romans used cement for many buildings (see page 97), but marble was also used in some of their most important structures. Some of this stone was imported from Greece,

Egypt, and Asia Minor, as well as taken from quarries on the Italian peninsula. Other building materials included wood, brick, and tile.

In *A History of the Roman People,* Allen Ward says, "Other than war, the business that . . . produced the biggest profits was finance, both public and private." This involved both lending money and making investments. Money lenders served some of the same purposes as modern banks, loaning money to business people looking to start a new venture or expand an old one. The borrower paid back the money with interest.

One type of investment opportunity was known as tax farming. During the Republic, people known as *publicani* collected taxes on behalf of the Roman government in parts of the provinces. They paid the government for this right and then kept what they collected. *Publicani* also won contracts to build public buildings. *Publicani* raised money to start their businesses by selling shares. They offered investors a percentage of the profits they made, based on how much money the investors risked. Today, most large companies also sell shares to outside investors.

Life in the City

City life in Roman times was lively, although it was often uncomfortable or dangerous. The wealthy owned their own large homes, with rooms centered around an open inner court called an atrium. Several generations of a family, along with slaves, often lived together. Typical workers and the poor lived in rented rooms or apartments. The apartments were usually located in buildings up to three stories tall. Renters often shared kitchens and bathrooms. In general, Romans of all classes did not have the same kind of privacy most Westerners expect in their homes today.

The rooms in apartment buildings tended to be small and dark. Some of the buildings were not well made, and wooden ones burned quickly if a fire broke out. Cicero was a landlord as well as a politician. Jo-Ann Shelton's *As the Romans Did* quotes a letter he wrote to a friend: "Two of my build-

CONNECTIONS >>>>>>>>>>>>>

From Urbs to Suburbs

The Latin word for city is *urbs*. That word is at the root of the English word *urban*, which describes anything related to a city. A related word is *suburb*, which literally means "near the city." That word has been used in English for hundreds of years to describe a town that is near a city. In more recent times, *suburb* led to *suburbia*, referring to the lifestyle of the suburbs, which is usually marked by a degree of wealth and leisure that most urban residents do not enjoy.

Water, Water Everywhere
This Roman aqueduct was built by the emperor Trajan to bring water to the Spanish city of Segovia. The Romans considered fresh, running water to be a necessity, and had the engineering skills to make it a reality throughout their empire.

ings have fallen down, and the rest have large cracks. Not only the tenants, but even the mice have moved out!"

With so many people jammed into one area, cities present certain discomforts and dangers that are not as common on farms or in small towns. That fact was as true in Roman times as it is today. Roman cities could be noisy. If diseases broke out, they could spread quickly. So could fires in city blocks made up of wooden buildings. During the Republic, Rome did not have a public fire department, although Augustus created a fire brigade manned by freed slaves. Some other cities also had associations of men who put out fires. The emperor Trajan preferred to buy fire fighting equipment that property owners could use when a fire broke out. He feared that a full-time fire department would develop into a political organization that might stir up trouble, especially in a provincial city.

Despite the risks of city life, Roman citizens also enjoyed what could be considered modern conveniences. With their talent for engineering, the Romans built huge structures called aqueducts that brought water into the cities. Large stone arches supported a covered passage that carried the water long distances. The water flowed into public fountains, where most people took what they needed for their daily activities. A few wealthy people had water piped directly into their homes. In modern times, this kind of indoor plumbing was not common until the 19th century. The Romans also built sewer systems that took waste out of the city. Slaves entered access holes to clean the sewers. In his *Geography*, the Greek author Strabo (c. 60 B.C.E.–c. 24 C.E.) noted that some sewers were so large that they "have room in some places for hay wagons to drive through them" (as quoted in Jo-Ann Shelton's *As the Romans Did*).

The Role of Religion

From the earliest days of Rome, religion played a key role in families and in the larger community. Roman religion was focused on daily life in the present, not a future afterlife in a perfect heaven. The Romans believed everything in nature had a spirit associated with it, and so did human-made items and activities—a house or even a doorway had a spirit associated with it, as did such essential acts as planting and harvesting crops. Romans set up altars where they made sacrifices or prayed to these spirits, with the goal of winning their blessing. Good spirits would help the Romans live happy and productive lives, while bad spirits, such as the one within a lightning bolt, could destroy property or kill a person.

In the early days of Rome, the father of a family was responsible for carrying out the religious rituals that

CONNECTIONS >>>>>>>>>>>>>

Ancient Water Works

Unlike many Mediterranean cities, Rome today has a constant supply of fresh, clean drinking water brought down from the hills through a system of pipes and aqueducts that has changed little from the time of the empire. When the city's wells were no longer sufficient to meet the needs of the ancient Romans, aqueducts were built to bring water form surrounding hills. The first aqueduct, the Aqua Appia, was built in 312 B.C.E.

Some aqueducts were more than 50 miles long. Water from a spring in the hills was collected in a reservoir to build up pressure. Then it flowed downhill all the way into the city, so there was no need for pumping (which would not have been possible). Water flowed through underground channels when it cut through high ground, and raised aqueducts maintained a constant gradient for carrying the water over low ground. The aqueducts were covered water channels supported by arches, all made of cut stone.

pleased the spirits. As Rome grew, political leaders took on the role of priests, trying to win favor with the gods for the entire community. Rome had a state religion—an official religion supported by the government. Priests were government officials, and the emperors built temples and paid for religious ceremonies.

During the monarchy, the Roman king was the chief priest. Later, most of the priests were elected officials, and a politician might run for the consul one year and the priesthood the next. Starting with Julius Caesar,

CONNECTIONS >>>>>>>>>>>>>>>>>>>>>>>>>>>>>>

The Roman Gods Today

Many Roman (and Greek) gods are familiar today, even if people do not realize their connection to Rome. A long list of English words have their roots in the gods' names. For example, the name of the god of war, Mars, led to the month of March, the planet Mars, and the word *martial*, which describes anything relating to war. Most of the planets in Earth's solar system are named for Roman gods. The word *volcano* comes from Vulcan, a Roman god who harnessed fire to make things for the other gods. The Romans thought Vulcan lived inside Mount Etna, a volcano in Sicily. The metal mercury is named for the god of the same name, who was a quick messenger for the other gods, as well as something of a trickster. People are sometimes called *mercurial* if they change their views quickly or are hard to pin down. Other examples include Fortuna, the goddess of luck, whose name appears in the English word *fortune*, and Juventas, the god of youth. His name is related to the Latin word for youth, *juventus*, and led to the English word *juvenile*.

Roman gods and myths have also appeared in Western art and literature throughout history. Many classic paintings, especially during the period of the Renaissance in Europe, show Roman gods and goddesses. One famous painting is *The Birth of Venus*, by Sandro Botticelli (1445–1510), which is often reproduced today on posters and cards. Many works by William Shakespeare, one of the greatest playwrights in the English language, make references to the Roman gods as a way of describing human behavior. From elementary school through college, students still read about the Greek and Roman gods and ancient and modern stories that refer to them.

Businesses also turn to the Roman myths, using the gods' names for their products. Some popular car models include Mercury, Saturn (the Roman version of Cronus, the father of the Olympians), and Aurora (the goddess of the dawn). Apollo has been used by several companies for their products, including a watchmaker and a computer company.

most Roman rulers also held the position of *pontifex maximus*, or chief priest. As such, the emperor made sacrifices as offerings to the gods at important festivals.

The most important women in Rome's religious life were the Vestal Virgins. Chosen as young girls, these daughters of patrician families pledged never to have sexual relations. The position was highly respected in Rome, and the government paid for all of the Vestal Virgins' living expenses. They spent their time watching over several important religious sites. A virgin who broke her vow not to have sex was buried alive.

Magistrates, generals, and emperors often based their decisions on auspices, or signs that seemed to suggest the gods supported certain actions. Specially trained people known as augurs interpreted the flight of birds or studies the entrails (guts) of slaughtered animals to look for these signs. Ignoring a sign or showing disrespect to sacred items was considered bad luck. The historian Suetonius, in *The Twelve Caesars,* describes how a Roman admiral threw chickens into the sea when they refused to eat. The birds were sacred, and the admiral's actions must have angered the gods, the Romans believed, since he lost his next battle.

Through the influence of the Greeks and Etruscans, the Romans began to anthropomorphize their spirits (give them human traits). Certain local gods were associated with similar Greek gods. The most important Roman gods corresponded to the major Greek gods said to live on Mount Olympus and known as the Olympians. The Roman god Jupiter, for example, who ruled everything above Earth, was identified with the most powerful Greek Olympian, Zeus. Venus, the goddess of love, was identified with the Greek goddess Aphrodite. A few gods had the same name in both Greek and Roman religions. The most important of these was Apollo, the god of the sun, who ruled over poetry, music, and medicine.

The roles of specific gods in human affairs sometimes changed over time. In the early days, the most important gods were associated with agriculture, since farming was so crucial to daily life. Both Jupiter and Mars started out this way: Jupiter provided the rain and light that made crops grow, while Mars watched over Roman crops and field animals. Eventually Jupiter was seen as god of specific cities, including Rome itself, and the god who ensured Rome's triumphs in war. Mars also became associated with war, sharing the traits of the Greek war god, Ares.

There were also goddesses. Juno, Jupiter's wife, was said to protect women, while Minerva was the goddess of wisdom. A god or goddess might have several roles and several names. Diana (originally an ancient Italian goddess of the forest) became the goddess of fertility, of virgin girls, and the moon. She was also known as Luna, the Latin word for moon, and Juno Lucina. When praying to a god, the Romans often said, "Hallowed be thy name, whatever name it is that you prefer," (as quoted in Shelton). That way, if they forgot one of the names, they would not offend the god.

The gods also included real Romans who were deified. After his death, Julius Caesar was worshiped as a god, and Augustus and several emperors after him were also deified. In some parts of the eastern empire, provincials worshiped the emperors as gods while they were still alive. The Roman government did not encourage this, but it did not try to stop it either, because the practice helped strengthen loyalty to the empire in distant regions. In general, the Romans let conquered people worship any way they chose, as long as they did not deny the role of the official state religion and the accepted gods.

Borrowing Gods

The Greeks were not the only people who influenced Roman religion. As the empire spread to Egypt and Asia Minor, the Romans adopted some gods from those regions. One of the earliest foreign gods accepted in Rome was Cybele. This goddess from Asia Minor was associated with nature and was sometimes called the Great Mother. While battling Carthage in 205 B.C.E., Roman officials tried to win her favor. Rituals devoted to her and her husband, Attis, featured wild outdoor dancing and priests cutting their own bodies.

In some cases foreign gods were associated with existing Roman gods. For example, Sulis, a Celtic god worshiped in Britain, was associated with Minerva, and the Syrian god Baal was linked to Jupiter. Other times, the new gods remained distinct and were given their own position of importance in the state religion.

Some of the new gods were worshiped in what were called mystery cults because believers did not talk about the details of their faith and its ceremonies. They took part in these cus while still practicing the state religion. The mystery cults offered a more direct experience with a god's spiritual power, and some of the cults promised eternal life. The mystery cult of the goddess Isis came from Egypt. Starting in the first century B.C.E., Rome tried to ban it, but people continued to worship Isis, and the emperor Caligula added her to the state religion. Another cult centered around the Parthian god Mithras. He was associated with the sun, and his followers believed they would live forever.

WINNING OVER A GOD

While fighting in foreign lands, the Romans sometimes asked their enemies' gods to give Rome aid. In return, the Romans promised to honor the foreign god by building temples and holding public games.

Jews in the Empire

Compared to other foreign religions within the Roman Empire, Judaism had a unique position. Unlike the Greeks, Romans, and other Mediterranean peoples, Jews worshiped just one god, with strict rules on how to worship that god and live daily life. Those rules included the rejection of all Roman gods. Centered in Judaea, Jews had practiced their religion for centuries before the rise of Rome. In 64 B.C.E. the Jews in Judaea came under Roman influence, and some eventually settled in Rome and other parts of the empire.

At first Roman officials let the Jews practice their faith without forcing them to accept the Roman gods. Gradually, however, some Romans distrusted the Jews because they did not also practice the state religion. Tiberius cracked down on the practice of Judaism in Rome. According to Suetonius, in *The Twelve Caesars*, Tiberius ordered all Jews "to burn their religious [clothes] and other accessories. . . . Jews of military age were moved to unhealthy regions . . . those too old or young to serve—including non-Jews who had adopted similar beliefs—were expelled from the City and threatened with slavery if they defied the order."

In Judaea, the Jews rebelled against Roman rule several times, fighting for their political independence and religious freedom. During the first revolt, from 66 to 70, the Romans destroyed the Jewish temple in Jerusalem. Starting around 129, Hadrian announced new limits on the practice of Judaism and planned to build a Roman-style city where Jerusalem stood. Those actions led to a second revolt in 132, which also ended with a Roman victory.

The Rise of Christianity

During the first century C.E., a new mystery cult emerged in the east with roots in Judaism. Around 29, Roman officials in Judaea presided over the crucifixion of a Jew known as Jesus. Before his death, Jesus had gathered followers while preaching a philosophy of love and the promise of life after death, if people accepted the Jewish god. Some of Jesus' teachings, however, contradicted accepted Jewish beliefs, which angered some of the Jewish leaders in Judaea.

Some of Jesus' followers claimed he was the Messiah. In Judaism, the Messiah is the person God has sent to unite the Jews and introduce an era of peace and prosperity. In Greek, the most common language in the eastern half of the Roman Empire, Jesus was called Christos, or "anointed one." After Jesus' death, his closest followers said that Jesus rose from

THE DIASPORA

One result of the failed Jewish revolts was the continued movement of Jews out of their traditional homeland, a process called the Diaspora. This movement of Jews into other lands had begun centuries before, when the Assyrians and Babylonians attacked the Jews in Judea. Under the Romans, however, the Diaspora carried the Jews farther away from the eastern Mediterranean. For the first time, sizable Jewish communities appeared in what is now Germany, Spain, France, northern Italy, and Dalmatia. After the fall of Rome, Jews continued to play a role in the social, economic, and artistic life of Europe.

his grave and ascended into heaven, a sign that he was the son of God. Based on Jesus' teachings and the writings of his disciples, a new faith emerged: Christianity.

Greek-speaking Jews and non-Jews who accepted that Jesus was the son of God began spreading Christianity throughout the Roman Empire. Paul, one of the most important early Christians and a Roman citizen, made four journeys to try to convert Romans to this new faith. The Roman emperors, however, disliked the Christians and their ideas. Like the Jews, the Christians would not accept the Roman gods, because they believed in just one God and the importance of his son, Jesus. And even more than the Jews, the Christians actively tried to recruit new members. The Christians also seemed to threaten public order, because they said all people were equal in God's eyes. This message appealed to the empire's poor, and emperors did not want large groups of people meeting and discussing ideas that might challenge the position of the rich and powerful in Rome.

For several centuries the Roman emperors persecuted the Christians—some more so than others. They denied them their legal rights, banned their religious ceremonies, and sometimes killed them. Nero blamed the great fire of 64 on the Christians. The historian Tacitus, in his annals, described how the Christians were "wrapped in the skin of animals…[and] torn apart by wild dogs, or nailed to crosses, or set on fire and burned alive to provide light at night, when the daylight had faded" (as quoted in

CONNECTIONS >>>>>>>>>>>>

Roman Festivals

The largest public celebrations in Rome through most of the Republic were religious festivals. These festivals featured public prayers and the sacrificing of animals to guarantee that particular gods continued to bless the Romans. One of the most important festivals was Lupercalia, celebrated on February 15. The rituals involved were supposed to purify Rome and make women fertile. After the rise of Christianity, church officials could not end the popular and deeply entrenched Lupercalia festival, so they associated it with a new Christian festival in honor of the Virgin Mary, the mother of Jesus Christ. Some historians also suggest that Valentine's Day has some roots in Lupercalia, because the Roman festival was associated with marriage and childbirth, leading to the modern holiday tied to romance and love.

Saturnalia was another major Roman festival. Held from December 17 through 23, the week-long celebration marked the shortest day of the year and honored the god Saturn. Businesses closed and everyone attended a public feast. At home, families cooked special meals and exchanged gifts, and for one day masters changed places with their slaves. As with Lupercalia, the Christian church merged some of these activities into a Christian holiday, Christmas. Some of that holiday's traditions, such as exchanging gifts, trace their roots to Saturnalia.

Jo-Ann Shelton's *As the Romans Did*). Christians who died this way, still proclaiming their faith, were known as martyrs, and believed they were assured a place in heaven. Despite ongoing persecution, the Christians continued to practice their faith, often meeting secretly in private homes.

By the start of the fourth century, Christianity had survived persecutions and emerged as major religion in the empire. Believers built large churches and held services in the open, instead of meeting privately. By this time, the Roman Empire was split in half, with an eastern and a western emperor (see page 52). In 311 Galerius (d. 311), the emperor in the east, said he would tolerate the open practice of Christianity. The next year Constantine, the western emperor, asked for Jesus Christ's help in a battle. When he won, Constantine gave some of the credit to Christ, and later converted to Christianity. He also granted legal privileges to Christians, although he did not ban non-Christian religions. Under the next few emperors, Christianity became the state religion, but the old faiths did not disappear completely.

The early Christian Church was led by men called bishops. They oversaw the religious activities in major cities and the surrounding towns. The most important bishops were based in five cities: Rome, Alexandria (in Egypt), Antioch (in Syria), Constantine's new capital city of Constantinople (in today's Turkey), and Jerusalem. Because of Rome's role as the former imperial capital, the Roman bishop was considered the "first among equals."

Centuries after the fall of Rome, in 1054, the Christian church split roughly along the lines of the old east-west division in the Empire. The western half of the Church, centered in Rome, used Latin as its official language and became today's Roman Catholic Church. The eastern half, based in Constantinople, spoke Greek and became the Orthodox (or Eastern Orthodox) Church.

Old Gods and New
The old Roman Forum is today ringed by Catholic churches, many of which incorporate marble columns from the old temples built for the Roman gods.

CHAPTER 6

Roman Art, Science, and Culture

AS WITH POLITICS AND RELIGION, ROMAN ART, SCIENCE, AND culture were heavily influenced by other peoples, especially the Greeks. Starting in the third century B.C.E., many Romans promoted the Hellenization of Roman culture. They borrowed ideas and sometimes literally stole Greek art–in 264 B.C.E., the Romans took 2,000 statues from a Greek city and erected them in a forum.

One of the earliest Greek influences was on architecture. The Greeks who settled in the southern part of the Italian peninsula brought their native styles with them, and the Etruscans and Romans copied those styles. Greek architecture featured columns, especially in public buildings such as temples and forums. The Romans improved on the Greek designs by introducing new building techniques. Better cement and the use of large, wide arches called vaults enabled the Romans to construct buildings with high ceilings that did not need columns to support their weight. The Romans also adapted a Greek building style called the basilica, in which the columns were placed inside, rather than outside a building. The Romans used these large basilicas as public meeting halls. Modern basilicas with a similar design are used as Roman Catholic churches.

The Romans used vaults and domes to create large indoor spaces in their public buildings. The greatest example is the Pantheon in Rome, built around 125 and still standing today. The building's large, open inner space has a high dome arching overhead. A hole in the center of the dome lets light into the building.

Another large, famous Roman structure was the Colosseum, which opened in 80. Also called the Flavian amphitheater, this large, oval stadium could hold about 50,000 people. It was built in rows of arches, set one

OPPOSITE
Art As History
This detail from Trajan's column shows Roman soldiers assisting the wounded. Emperor Trajan erected the 100-foot column in 113 to celebrate his victory over Dacia. Relief carvings wind all the way up the length of the column.

Marvel of Architecture
The Pantheon is now a Catholic church. The vast dome was cast by pouring concrete over a temporary wooden framework.

on top of the other. The Colosseum had no roof, but canvas covers could be pulled over the top that kept the rain and sun off the sections where the important people sat.

The Romans used large wooden cranes to lift heavy building materials. The cranes were powered by huge treadwheels in which slaves walked around, making the wheel turn. The wheel pulled a rope that was tied to the heavy building block, lifting the block as high as the arm of the crane.

The emperors erected huge buildings so they could impress Romans and visitors with their wealth and power. The Romans also took their building styles to the lands they ruled. Ruins of Roman amphitheaters and temples still stand today in North Africa, Asia Minor, and Europe. Greco-Roman styles also appear today in many government buildings across the Western world. In the United States, such buildings as the National Gallery of Art in Washington, D.C., show this influence.

Sculpture and Painting

When they did not steal Greek statues outright, the Romans often made copies of Greek works. Over time, however, Roman artists began to develop their own forms. Roman statues stressed realism—the goal was to make the sculpture look as much as possible like the model it represented. This goal had its roots in family life, because families wanted statues that portrayed accurate images of their dead ancestors, to honor their memory. Roman sculptors focused on busts, which show a person from the shoulders up. The artist tried to capture every wrinkle or flaw in a person's face, rather than trying to make them look perfect.

Another Roman specialty in sculpture was the relief. Relief images emerge from a flat or curved background, such as the side of a building. One of the most famous examples of a Roman relief is on Trajan's Column, which the emperor built in Rome in 113 to celebrate his victory over Dacia. The relief images show scenes from the Dacian battles, winding

Roman Concrete

In the center of modern Rome's business district stands the Pantheon, which means "temple of all the gods." This huge domed temple was built by the emperor Hadrian (118–125) and was converted to a Christian church during the Middle Ages. Its basic shape—a large domed structure with a classical portico in front (a portico is a kind of porch, in this case a triangular roof supported by many columns)—has influenced architecture to the present day. Many government buildings and monuments, including the Jefferson Memorial in Washington, D.C., use this basic shape.

But what makes the Pantheon really amazing is that its massive dome, 140 feet high and the same distance across, is made of concrete—concrete that has withstood the elements for almost 2,000 years and that includes no steel reinforcing, which is the way we hold modern concrete structures together.

Roman concrete consisted of three parts: a pasty, hydrated lime; volcanic ash from the town of Pozzuoli in Italy; and fist-sized pieces of rock. What made Roman concrete so special is the chemistry of pozzolan ash. People had long been using an inferior form of concrete, using plaster, lime, rocks and water, for small building projects. But the mixture was very thin and difficult to work with, and it did not last long. The Romans discovered that mixing a little volcanic ash in a fine powder with the moist lime made a durable concrete that could be submerged in water. In fact, some of the complex chemistry of ancient concrete matches the chemical formula of modern concrete.

But chemistry alone will not make good concrete. The Romans hand mixed their components in a mortar box with very little water to give a nearly dry composition, carried it to the construction site in baskets, placed it over a previously prepared layer of rock pieces or a wooden frame, and then pounded it into place. This close packing reduced the need for water in the mix, and water is a source of bubbles and weak spots. Pounding also produces a better bond. This is the reason the concrete in modern roads is compacted with a giant roller during their construction.

The development of strong, durable concrete enabled architects to develop exciting, original designs, including domes, for centuries to come. It freed them from the limitations of rectangular stone blocks or bricks and the expense of carved stone. Concrete is lighter than stone, enabling architects to be more flexible in their designs. And the fact that it is so easily molded when wet makes it ideal for decorative elements on buildings.

up the column about 100 feet. If the relief sculpture were laid out in a straight line, it would stretch about 650 feet. Trajan's Column can still be seen in Rome today.

Roman painters usually worked on the walls and ceilings of homes, rather than on canvases. The artists typically used bright colors, and they painted a wide range of subjects: scenes from everyday life, buildings, gods, and scenes from myths. Some Roman paintings can be seen today on the buildings at Pompeii. Other examples have been taken down from their original sites and moved to museums.

Another Greek art style popular in Rome was mosaics. Tiny colored pieces of glass and stone were used to create pictures or patterns, usually on the floors of buildings, though sometimes on the walls. The best mosaic makers could almost exactly copy the details captured in a painting.

Roman Literature

As Greece's influence on Rome grew, wealthy Romans learned to read, write, and speak Greek. The once-powerful Greek city-states had developed sophisticated forms of drama, poetry, and philosophy. The Romans wanted to read these works and produce their own. At the same time, educated Greeks came to Rome and translated some Greek writings into Latin. Around 240 B.C.E., a Greek teacher named Livius Andronicus (c. 284–c. 204 B.C.E.) translated the Greek epic story *The Odyssey*. He also turned several Greek plays into Latin productions. Livius Andronicus's efforts marked the start of Roman literature. Other writers soon followed with original works written in Latin, both poetry and drama.

The most successful Roman literature of the Republic was drama. Plautus (c. 254–184 B.C.E.) wrote more than 130 comedies, and several of them are still read and performed today. The characters and plots in his works influenced the writers of the modern musical *A Funny Thing Happened on the Way to the Forum*, which still plays on stages across the United States. A popular movie of the play appeared in 1966.

To the Greeks and Romans, history was an important form of literature. The first major historians included Polybius and Cato the Elder. Later in the Republic, Julius Caesar wrote important historical works, as did Sallust (c. 86–c. 35 B.C.E.). Cato the Elder was also known for his writings on law and rhetoric (the art of persuasion through public speaking). Rome highly praised its orators. Another famous master of rhetoric was Seneca the Elder (c. 55 B.C.E.–c. 40 C.E.). He published exercises

LIVY

The Golden Age also produced one notable historian, Livy. His work was not always accurate, because he usually tried to present Rome in the best light, but his writing style used poetic and dramatic touches that made his books enjoyable to read. He is one of the major sources for modern historians studying the foreign battles of the early and middle years of the Republic.

Cicero

Marcus Tullius Cicero's life coincided with the decline and fall of the Roman Republic, and he was an important actor in many of the significant political events of his time. His writings are now a valuable source of information to us about those events, and his literary legacy had enormous influence in the West through the mid-15th century.

Cicero began his political career as an orator and lawyer. He was elected to each of the principle Roman offices on his first try. Having held office automatically made him a member of the Roman Senate.

During his term as consul in 63 B.C.E. he was responsible for unraveling and exposing a conspiracy to take over the Roman state by force. Five of the conspirators were put to death without trial on Cicero's orders. Later, during the political struggles between Julius Caesar and Pompey, this action was used as an excuse to send Cicero—a stanch supporter of the Republic—into exile.

After less than two years of exile, he was allowed to return to Rome but not to take part in politics. When Caesar was murdered in 44 B.C.E., Cicero hoped the Republic would be restored. He made a series of speeches to the Senate, known as the Philippics, that made him many political enemies, and the following year he, his brother, and his nephew were killed while trying to flee Italy.

Cicero felt philosophy should serve politics, and his philosophical writings sought to defend the Roman Republic. The politicians of his time, he believed, were corrupt and no longer possessed the virtuous character that had been the main attribute of Romans in the early days. This loss of virtue was, he believed, the cause of the Republic's difficulties. He said the Republic could only be renewed if the Roman elite would improve their character and commit themselves first and foremost to individual virtue and social stability.

Philosophy was an activity in which Greece (and especially Athens) still held the lead. To make philosophy more accessible to the Romans, Cicero drew on an idealized version of Roman history to provide examples of appropriate conduct. He also created many new Latin words for Greek philosophical concepts, including the Latin words that eventually gave us the English *words morals, property, individual, science, image*, and *appetite*. Cicero also summarized in Latin many of the beliefs of the primary Greek philosophical schools of the time, which is how we know about them today.

While he is not as widely read today, in previous centuries he was considered one of the great philosophers of the ancient era. Probably the most notable example of his influence is St. Augustine's claim that it was Cicero's *Hortensius* (an exhortation to philosophy, the text of which is unfortunately lost) that turned him away from his sinful life and toward philosophy, and ultimately, to God.

The Latin Alphabet

Like so much of Rome's culture, its alphabet had Greek and Etruscan roots. Today, most of the Western world still uses the Latin alphabet, with some minor changes. The Romans did not have the letters J, U, or W. J evolved out of the letter I, and some English words that begin with J started with an I in their Latin form. For example, the Latin *ius*, or law, became the root for such English words as *judge* and *judicial*. Both U and W developed out of V. In Latin, V could be spoken with either a W or U sound. So, for example, in Roman times *ius* would have been written as *ivs*.

in both Greek and Latin that students used to sharpen their oration skills.

The reign of Augustus marked what modern historians call the Golden Age of Roman literature. The noted writers of the Republic focused on drama and non-fiction, but the writers of this Golden Age were mostly poets. They often wrote about similar themes, especially the glory of Rome in the past and its new-found glory under Augustus. Most famous of these poets today is Virgil (70–19 B.C.E.). His *Aeneid* is the best-known version of the story of Aeneas, the legendary ancestor of Romulus. The poem describes how Aeneas was forced out of Troy, landed at Carthage, then finally settled in the Italian peninsula. Virgil wrote that Jupiter himself chose the Romans to achieve their great success:

> *A race shall rise*
> *All powerful . . . you will see them*
> *By virtue of devotion rise to glories*
> *Not men nor gods have known*

For centuries, until about 1900, every educated Westerner knew Virgil's work in its original form, since schools regularly taught Latin. The *Aeneid* is still read today, although usually in translation. Virgil's writing style and themes influenced many Roman writers and later English poets, such as John Spenser, William Shakespeare, and John Milton.

The other major poets of the Golden Age include Horace (65–8 B.C.E.) and Ovid (43 B.C.E.–17 C.E). Horace was famous for his short poems, called odes, which dealt with a variety of topics ranging from daily activities to philosophy. Among his memorable lines is this one, taken from his first book of odes: "It is sweet and honorable to die for one's country" (as quoted in *Barlett's Quotations*). That notion fit in well with the Roman value of sacrifice, especially for the state. Ovid is best remembered today for a series of books called *The Metamorphoses*. The poet traces the history of the world, up to the time of Julius Caesar, and provides information on the Greek gods and goddesses adopted by the Romans. For centuries, artists and writers used scenes from *The Metamorphoses* in their works, and in 2002, a staged version of some of these stories became a hit play in New York City.

Under Claudius and Nero, another group of talented writers emerged, though not as polished as the generation before them. Later literary critics called this period the Silver Age. Seneca the Younger (c. 4 B.C.E.–65 C.E.), was Nero's teacher. His many writings included tragic plays, essays, and a book on science. Seneca often focused on morality in his works. Another scientific writer was Pliny the Elder (23–79), who

CONNECTIONS >>>>>>>>>>>>>>>>>>>>>>>>>>>>>>>>

The Stoics

Marcus Aurelius, one of the five good emperors, was also known for his writing. His book *Meditations* reflects his interest in Stoic philosophy. Developed in Athens in the third century B.C.E., Stoicism got its name from the Stoa Poilike—Greek for "painted meeting hall"—the building where the founders of this philosophy met. The Greek Stoics called for the kind of values many Romans already accepted: self-discipline, hard work, and the need to follow traditions. In Rome, Stoics placed even more emphasis on doing one's duty in a disciplined way.

The Stoics believed the entire universe was made up of a single substance or spirit, and this spirit was the plan of how the universe would develop. This spirit was sometimes called God, Nature, or Fate. Another name for the spirit was Reason, and the Stoics argued that the only way to be happy was to use Reason, the power of the thinking mind, in every part of life. A person's rational mind, they said, was the same thing as Reason or God. The Stoics disliked strong emotions, since they kept people from following Reason. To be happy, humans had to stop worrying about the future or luck. They also had to remember that acquiring or losing wealth was not important; rather, people were measured by the good things they did in life. Students still study Stoicism as one approach to ethics, a branch of philosophy concerned with good and evil and how to live a moral life.

Today, the word *stoic* is used to describe people who do not become emotional during a crisis or who bear pain or distress with fortitude. They accept whatever happens to them and always do their duty. A stoic, however, is not necessarily a Stoic—that is, someone who follows the traditional Stoic philosophy.

wrote a long work on natural history. His nephew, Pliny the Younger, was also a writer. His letters provide modern historians with details about everyday Roman life. A noted poet of the Silver Age was known as Martial (c. 40–c. 103, his full name was Marcus Valerius Martialis), who wrote short, witty sayings called epigrams.

Roman literature declined during the Flavian Dynasty, then improved during the reign of the five good emperors (see page 40). Juvenal (c. 55–c. 130) was one of the better-known poets of his age. His specialty was satire—writing that uses sharp humor to criticize current social and political problems. Notable historians included Appian (d. c. 160), Tacitus, Suetonius, and Plutarch. A versatile writer of the era was Apuleius (c. 123–c. 180), who wrote about science and philosophy. Apuleius also wrote a novel, *The Metamorphoses*, which today is usually called *The Golden Ass*. The book's main character experiments with magic and turns himself into a donkey. This work is the only complete Latin novel from Roman times that survives today.

Entering the third century, Roman literature went into decline. The most important writers were historians, scientists, and philosophers. The leading philosopher was Plotinus (205–270), who based his ideas on the teachings of the ancient Greek philosopher, Plato (c. 427–347 B.C.E.). Plotinus taught that a single force, though not a god, created everything in the universe. His ideas are referred to as neoplatonism, a reference to the influence of Plato.

The rise of Christianity and its eventual dominance in the empire inspired a number of Christian writers who are still read today. One of the first was Tertullian (c. 160–240). He wrote about such topics as marriage and the soul from a Christian viewpoint, and he strongly attacked pagan beliefs. A leading later Christian writer was St. Augustine (354–430). His best-known works are his *Confessions* and *City of God*. Augustine's ideas still influence the Roman Catholic Church today.

CONNECTIONS >>>>>>>>>>>

Medical Language

As in today's legal world, Latin is a key part of the language of medicine. Many parts of the body have a formal name with Latin roots as well as a more common English name. The kneecap, for example, is the patella, which is also the Latin word for "shallow dish." The upper arm bone is called the humerus, the Latin word for "shoulder." The names of medical procedures and conditions also have their roots in Latin words. The names of different types of cancer often end in "noma," such as melanoma, a type of skin cancer. *Noma* is also the Latin version of the Greek word *nome*, which means "the spread of an ulcer."

Roman Medical Science

As with the arts, the Romans looked to the Greeks for ideas about science and technology. The Greeks were particularly strong in mathematics and the philosophy of science, and the Romans excelled in using science and engineering principles in practical ways.

One science that directly affected everyday life was medicine. The best doctors in Rome were Greek slaves or freedmen, and the most important medical works were written in Greek and then translated into Latin. Doctors and surgeons were important for the military, and some wealthy people hired their own personal doctors. Some women also served as doctors—one of the few professional jobs they could hold. Other women were midwives, who helped pregnant women give birth.

Greek doctors tried to use true science to find the cause and cure of illness. Romans mixed both scientific ideas and religious beliefs in their medicine, with most of the true science coming from the Greeks.

One of the greatest Greek doctors of during the Roman Empire was Galen (129–c. 200). He dissected animals to study how their bodies worked. Galen also did some dissection of dead humans, and some of his first medical experience came at the gladiatorial games, where he treated injured fighters. Later he served as the personal doctor of Marcus Aurelius. In light of today's medical knowledge, Galen's ideas were not always correct, but he influenced Western medicine for more than 1,000 years. For example, Galen argued that four bodily fluids shaped both health and personality, and that a doctor should try to balance these fluids—an idea doctors followed for centuries.

Some Roman medical practices and tools are not much different from ones used today. According to Peter James and Nick Thorpe, authors of *Ancient Inventions*, "Some of the instruments used by Roman doctors were of such superb quality that any modern surgeon would be proud to own them." For example, the Romans, like modern doctors, used special knives called scalpels to perform surgery. To amputate diseased limbs, they used heavy bone-cutting saws. At Pompeii archaeologists found forceps—tools used to hold or grasp delicate tissues—that were as precise as modern ones.

Roman doctors performed operations on the eyes to remove cataracts. At times, surgeons also drilled into patients' skulls, trying to cure headaches or other problems. If a patient lost a limb, doctors sometimes gave him or her an artificial one. A skeleton buried in Capua, Italy, had a fake leg made out of wood and bronze, and the patient probably also

BECOMING A DOCTOR
Unlike today, Roman doctors did not have to attend special schools or prove their skills in any way before going into business. Most learned their art by watching other doctors. Martial complained about this practice in his *Epigrams*. Martial wrote (as quoted in Jo-Ann Shelton's *As the Romans Did*) that the doctor Symmachus "brought 100 medical students with [him]. One hundred ice-cold hands poked and jabbed me. I didn't have a fever, Symmachus, when I called you—but I do now."

Go Figure

Scientists and engineers need math skills. The Romans borrowed their mathematics from the Greeks, and as in medicine, some of the best mathematicians in the Roman Empire were Greek or wrote in Greek. These include Ptolemy (c. 90–c. 168), who was also an astronomer. He was famous for a book that claimed—wrongly, as it later turned out—that the sun and planets revolved around the Earth.

For their numerals, Romans used letters from their alphabet: I=1, V=5, X=10, L=50, C=100, D=500

The numeral for 1,000 was originally C followed by I and a backward C, but later Latin scholars replaced this with the letter M. Numerals could be repeated up to three times to represent larger numbers: II, for example, is 2, and XXX is 30. A smaller numeral placed before a larger one meant the smaller amount was subtracted from the larger: IV, for example, is 4, and XC is 90.

Today, the Western world uses Arabic numerals, not Roman ones. In some instances, however, the Roman numerals are still used, such as to number sections or chapters in a book or distinguish among rulers with the same name. They are also sometimes used on coins, on the cornerstones of buildings and other places where people want to give the impression of grandeur and permanence.

wore a separate wooden foot at the bottom. To help reduce a patient's pain, Roman doctors used a variety of plant-based drugs, such as opium, henbane, and mandrake.

Engineering Feats

One of the great inventors of Roman times was Heron (dates unknown), who lived in Egypt during the first century. He used steam power to create toys with moving parts and doors that opened automatically. Another one of his inventions has been called the world's first steam engine, because it used the steam from boiling water to spin a metal ball. Modern jet engines use some of the same principles as this device for their extraordinary power, with heated gases spinning a metal fan. Heron also built what might be considered the world's first vending machine. People put a coin in the top and received a small cup of water.

Ancient Greek writers wrote about the gods using gold and other metals to make creatures that behaved as humans did. Over time, this idea led to the creation of automata—machines that move on their own. Heron made several automata. One was a self-moving stand that could carry small items. The movement of sand within the stand lowered a weight that was connected to wheels along several pulleys. As the weight moved, the wheels turned. The stands were used during plays to create a sense of magic, or to carry small automatic theaters that Heron also built. Again, weights and pulleys moved objects, this time small metal figures that looked like people and animals.

The Romans excelled as builders, and their engineering skills helped them make some of the largest and most complex grain mills ever known. The Romans needed huge amounts of grains to feed their armies and citizens, which required large mills that could grind the grains into flour. One of the largest was built near Arles, France, during the fourth century. An aqueduct carried water to eight pairs of waterwheels, which were located on both sides of the mill buildings. The turning wheels were connected by wooden gears to the large stones that ground the grains. Perhaps as much as 10 tons of flour or corn could be ground every day.

Romans also used waterwheels in their mining operations. For centuries, miners working below the ground had to deal with water flooding into the mines. The Romans built wheels with containers on them that scooped up the water as the wheel spun and dumped it on a slightly higher level. A series of wheels could remove the water from a mine almost 100 feet deep. People provided the power that turned the wheels—slaves walked on treads attached to the wheels' outer rims.

The mill operations at Arles show that the Romans used technology to guarantee a steady supply of food. In the fields of France, farmers used what may have been the world's first reaper, a machine that cuts down ripe grains. The Roman invention had a cart with a set of sharp blades across the front. A donkey, with a farmer behind it, pushed the cart through the field. The blades cut the grain, which then fell into the cart. A larger version of this reaping machine may have been pushed by oxen.

The Romans were the world's first people to build large fish farms. Farmers cut tanks out of rocks near the sea and raised such fish as sea bass and mullet, as well as shellfish, particularly oysters. Pathways called sluices carried seawater to and from the tanks, which could be as much as 115 feet long and 58 feet wide.

Public Entertainment

Some of Rome's greatest architects and engineers designed and built structures that were used for public entertainment. Races, gladiatorial games, sports, and theatrical performances were originally part of religious festivals. Over the centuries, the focus of these events changed, and they celebrated military triumphs and the empire's growing wealth. Emperors wanted to impress Roman citizens and earn their loyalty, and free entertainment was one way to accomplish this. At times, the emperors also used public entertainment to distract the poor from economic and social problems.

The oldest and most popular public event in Rome was chariot racing. The Romans and other ancient peoples used chariots in combat as well as sporting events. Roman races were held in a large, oval arena called a circus. The largest one in the empire was called the Circus Maximus, Latin for "largest race track." This arena in Rome could hold at least 150,000 spectators.

According to Roman legend, Romulus held the first chariot races shortly after founding the city of Rome, and the Circus Maximus was built on the same spot. By the end of the Republic, chariot racing was a highly developed professional sport. The drivers competed for one of four teams, distinguished by the color of their clothing: red, blue, green, or white. Groups of wealthy Romans owned the teams, paying for the horses and the drivers' training. Most drivers were slaves, and they received a small prize for their victories. Most of the money awarded to the victors went to the team owners.

The races usually featured chariots pulled by teams of two or four horses, with one driver. At times, the chariots crashed into each other, just as in today's car races. The drivers were often injured—and sometimes killed—in these collisions. Sidonius Apollinaris (c. 430–c. 480), a poet, described one of these crashes (as recorded in Jo-Ann Shelton's *As the Romans Did*), "[The driver's] horses lose their balance and fall. Their legs become tangled in the spinning chariot wheels. . . . The driver is hurled

CONNECTIONS >>>>>>>>>>>>

Colossal Colosseum

The Colosseum took its name from the Latin word *colossus*, which means "a giant statue." A huge statue of Nero stood near the stadium, giving it its nickname. The English word *colossal*, describing anything huge, has the same root. And today, many large arenas for sports and cultural events are sometimes called coliseums. Some modern coliseums, such as the Los Angeles Coliseum, were built to look like the original Colosseum in Rome.

Most of the original Colosseum still stands in Rome, and it is the largest imperial structure remaining in the city. Several complete Roman amphitheaters also still stand; the one in Arles, France, is used for bullfights.

The Colosseum was commissioned by Emperor Vespasian in 72. It had 80 entrance arches and room for 55,000 spectators.

The Heart of the Games
This mosaic of popular gladiators dates from the late third century. Their names are written beside them.

headlong out of the shattered chariot which then falls on top of him in a heap of twisted wreckage."

On race day, fans cheered wildly for their favorite team, often betting on the races. At times, fights broke out in the stands between groups of fans, as occasionally happens at modern sporting events. Emperors often attended the circus, and Nero even competed in some of the races, although most educated Romans did not approve of an emperor taking part in a public sport.

The Games

In earlier times, before most cities had permanent racetracks, wild animals were sometimes brought into the circus and fought each other to the death. Other times, humans stalked them in a public hunt. Chariot races and animal hunts were often a part of a larger event known as the games. The games also sometimes had animals that performed tricks for the crowds. The celebrations associated with games could last for a week. Admission to the games was free, with the Senate and public officials picking up the expense.

Over time the Romans built amphitheaters, such as the Colosseum, especially for the games. These arenas featured animal hunts and

107

CONNECTIONS >>>>>>>>>>>>

Entertainment in the Round

The Roman word *circus* came from the Greek word *kirkos*, meaning "ring." Like the Roman racetrack, the English word *circus* describes a round arena—in our case, where acrobats, clowns, animals, and other acts are performed. The Roman root of the word *circus* also appears in other English words, such as *circle* and *circumference* (the outer edge of a circle). And to *circumnavigate* is to travel around the world in a circle.

gladiatorial combat, which were too dangerous for the circus or other public spaces because the spectators were too close to the field. In the amphitheaters, the fans sat high above the fighting area. The arenas also had special underground cells to hold the animals. Sand in the middle of the arena helped soak up the blood shed by both animals and humans.

The first gladiatorial games were private events hosted by families to honor their dead. During the empire, the games became lavish public events. The gladiators were usually convicted criminals, slaves, or prisoners of war. A few gladiators volunteered to take part in the games. The gladiators went to special schools to learn how to fight with specific weapons. These included a three-forked spear called a trident and a net, which a gladiator used to ensnare his opponent.

As with the charioteers, fans rooted for particular gladiators, and sometimes threw money to the victors. Some slaves earned enough money this way to buy their freedom. The fights were not always to the death. Some matches ended in draws, and some losers survived the beating they took in the arena. The men who ran the games did not want each match to end in death because they could not afford to lose half their fighters in each day's combat, since they spent their own money to train the gladiators.

The losers in some gladiatorial combats appealed to the crowd for mercy. By putting their thumbs up or down, the fans indicated if the fighters should live or die. The emperor, who made the final decision, usually accepted the crowd's wishes. If the crowd put their thumbs down, the loser was immediately executed. Today, a thumbs-up sign still signals approval, while thumbs down indicates displeasure.

Another feature of the games was mock sea battles, first staged by Julius Caesar. At one time, historians thought the Romans somehow flooded the Colosseum and held the battles there, but they actually took place on artificial lakes in the city.

Although aspects of the games seem brutal and cruel today, most Romans accepted them as a valid form of entertainment. Violence went on in the society all the time: Owners beat slaves, fathers and teachers hit children, citizens without money were beaten if they committed certain crimes. In addition, Rome honored the military and the idea of using war to achieve wealth and power was completely accepted. In that climate, writes historian Jo-Ann Shelton, "People who themselves felt powerless and brutalized found some satisfaction in watching the infliction of pain on others." Still, some educated Romans did not approve of the games. Cicero, after attending an event where 600 lions were killed, wrote in a letter to a friend (also quoted in Shelton), "But what pleasure can a civilized man find when either a helpless human being is mangled by a very strong animal, or a magnificent animal is stabbed again and again with a hunting spear?"

The Theater

Animals and athletes were not the only entertainment in the Roman Empire. Theatrical performances in Rome dated to the fourth century B.C.E. By the end of the Republic, the Romans had built huge theaters with as many as 20,000 seats. During the games Romans were more likely to spend time at the theater than at the circus or the amphitheater.

Roman performers staged a variety of shows for their audiences. In the plays written by Roman and Greek authors, male actors performed all the roles, often wearing masks. These plays were popular with educated Romans. The poor and working classes usually preferred pantomime and mime shows, which often dealt with mythology and might feature nudity. Both men and women acted in these shows. In pantomime, the actors did not speak. Music played during the performance and the actors danced, similar to a ballet. Mime shows also featured dancing and music, but the actors spoke.

Comedy Tonight
This wall painting from Pompeii shows three actors in a comedy. The man on the left is wearing a mask that indicates he is a slave.

Like other parts of the games, a theatrical performance could feature grand spectacles. One of the devices designed by the inventor Heron (see page 104) was a small theater that rolled itself out in front of an audience. Automata inside the theater performed, then the whole theater rolled away. At performances featuring actors, producers might bring live animals on stage. One performance featured riders on horses, while another used hundreds of mules. Theatrical special effects included actors hanging above the stage on wires and popping out of trap doors in the floor. Both effects are still sometimes used in the theater today.

The Baths

Bathing is a part of daily life today that usually takes place in private. The Romans, however, built huge public baths that provided another form of public entertainment or recreation. Most Romans had to use public baths, since their homes did not have a bath.

Going to the baths was also a social event, since using the public baths gave people a chance to meet their friends. Most baths had a gym, and some also had a library and meeting rooms. Some historians have compared the public baths to a modern health club or community center.

The Baths of Bath
Many bath houses built by the Romans are still standing, including this one in England in a town named Bath.

The baths were so popular that by the fourth century, the city of Rome had almost 1,000 of them.

A typical session at the bath started with some physical activity in a gymnasium, such as jogging or weightlifting. Bathers could also swim. The actual bathing took place in a series of pools, with separate baths for men and women. In between dips in the water, bathers received massages using different oils. One service offered at the baths was hair plucking, in which attendants pulled out any unwanted hairs on the bathers' bodies. Bathers could also buy food and drinks at the baths' snack bars.

The emperors built some of the baths in Rome and the provinces, and a few of them still stand today, although they are not used for bathing. In England, the Romans built a huge bath in a town called Aquae Sulis (*aquae* is a form of the Latin word for water, and Sulis was a Celtic water goddess). The water came from nearby mineral springs. Today, the town is called Bath and parts of the Roman buildings still stand.

Private Entertainment

Along with public entertainment and recreation, some Romans—mostly the rich—enjoyed entertaining at home in private groups. The wealthy opened their homes to friends and important guests and served fancy banquets. At these private parties, guests usually sprawled out on couches, and during nice weather the meals were served outside. These banquets could last as long as 10 hours, with many courses. The entertainment might also include music, dancing, and poetry readings.

Romans with less money could not afford to entertain in their homes, but they still wanted to eat and drink with friends. Many joined associations that the Romans called *collegia* (the root of the English word *college*). The *collegia* were like today's social clubs, in which members pay dues. Eating and drinking together was the focus of monthly meetings. Some *collegia* were only for the members of a specific profession, others were centered around shared religious beliefs or where the members lived. One type of *collegia* was known as a funeral club. Members paid dues and when they died the club paid for their funeral.

Children also had their own entertainment. Indoors, they played board games. Just as today, they might also play with dolls or shoot marbles. Outdoors, Roman children played games similar to leap frog and hide-and-seek. Most children, however, did not have much time for playing. In poor families, children were expected to help with the farm or perform other chores starting at an early age.

RUNNING HOT AND COLD

Roman bathers went through a routine when they used baths. After completing their exercises, they went into the *tepidarium*, which held a pool of warm water. The next step was the *calidarium*, filled with hot water heated by a furnace. Finally, the last bath came in the cold waters of the *frigidarium*. The names of three different baths show some similarities to modern English words. *Tepid* is used to describe a mildly warm temperature—or a person's mild reaction to some event. *Calor*, the Latin word for heat, can be seen in the word *calidarium*, and is also the root for *calorie*, an English word for a measure of heat. *Frigid* is an English word for a cold temperature or a person with a cold personality, and a form of the word also appears in *refrigerator*.

Epilogue

JUSTINIAN FAILED TO RESTORE THE OLD ROMAN EMPIRE (SEE page 59), but its traditions continued in the "barbarian" west, the Greek east, and the language and thought of the Roman Catholic Church. European history continued to be shaped by political, legal, and artistic ideas that reflected the Greco-Roman culture developed under the Roman emperors.

For centuries after the last western emperor lost power, other European rulers tried to suggest that they somehow had inherited something of the Roman tradition. In Gaul the Franks created their own kingdom, forming the basis of modern-day France. One Frankish king, Charlemagne (742–814), extended the kingdom into parts of Germany and the Italian peninsula, and in 800 he received a new title. The Frankish writer Einhard (c. 770–840), in *Life of Charlemagne*, writes, "Charles . . . went to Rome, to set in order the affairs of the Church, which were in great confusion, and passed the whole winter there. It was then that he received the titles of Emperor and Augustus." For a time, the emperors of Constantinople considered Charlemagne their equal, and together they and the Frankish king ruled over most of the old Roman Empire. Latin was still the official language in the west, and Charlemagne's scholars looked to Greco-Roman (sometimes called classical) models for their writings.

Charlemagne's empire died, but it was replaced by another state that called itself the Holy Roman Empire. A German ruler named Otto (936–973), from the region called Saxony, united several central European states and parts of the Italian peninsula under his rule. This new Holy Roman Empire lasted until the 12th century, although later historians commented that it was neither holy, nor Roman, nor truly an empire.

OPPOSITE
The Picture of Power
Francois Gerard (1770–1837) painted this portrait of Napoleon in his coronation robes. The laurel wreath on his head and the eagle on his staff are both Roman symbols of power.

Still, in the 19th century, British historian James Viscount Bryce wrote (as found in David Thompson's *The Idea of Rome*) that the German emperors had "a loftiness of spirit and a sense of duty to the realm they ruled which recalls the old Roman type."

The idea of carrying on the Roman tradition also spread eastward. Through their contact with the Byzantine Empire, Russian rulers embraced the Orthodox religion and Greco-Roman political ideas. During the 15th century, Ivan the Great (1440–1505) took the Byzantine title *autocrator* and called himself *czar*—the Russian form of caesar. Legends circulated in Russia that Ivan's family traced its roots to the brother of the emperor Augustus. And at times Ivan referred to his capital, Moscow, as the "third Rome," after the original and the "New Rome" of Constantinople.

As recently as the 19th and 20th centuries, European rulers looked to ancient Rome for inspiration. Napoleon Bonaparte (1769–1821) named himself emperor of France in 1804 while trying to conquer large parts of Europe and Egypt. For a time he called himself first consul, and as emperor he wore a laurel wreath made of gold, similar to the laurel wreaths worn in Roman times by emperors, and victorious soldiers and athletes. Napoleon also encouraged French artists to copy Roman styles of art. Benito Mussolini (1883–1945), who seized power in Italy during the 1920s, also looked to ancient Rome; Mussolini tried to convince his people they could rebuild the past glory of the Roman Empire. And in Germany during the 1930s, Adolf Hitler (1889–1945) called his government the Third Reich, or third empire, since it followed the Holy Roman Empire of the Middle Ages and a

CONNECTIONS >>>>>>>>>>>>

Enduring Symbols

Under Marius, toward the end of the Roman Republic, all the Roman legions used an eagle as their standard (symbol). Eagles stood for strength and were associated with the god Jupiter. The eagle was an important symbol to the Roman emperors as well, and it lasted after the fall of the western Empire. In the east, a double-headed eagle represented the Byzantine government, and later the German emperors and the Russian czars adopted a similar symbol. Napoleon, Mussolini, and Hitler also used Roman eagles as symbols of their rule.

Mussolini added another touch from Rome's imperial past: He reintroduced the letters "SPQR," which stood for the Latin words *Senatus Populusque Romanus*—"the Senate and the People of Rome." Beginning in the Republic, these letters appeared on all official government documents. Today, several computer games set in Roman times are called SPQR, and the letters are sometimes used as a symbol for web sites connected to Roman history. The letters also appear on all the manhole covers in Rome.

more recent German empire, whose rulers were called kaisers–the German form of caesar.

Influence on Art and Education

Rome's achievements in art and education–along with what the Romans learned from the Greeks–also lived on long past the fall of the western Empire. The four or five centuries after this fall were sometimes called the Dark Ages. Except for monks, few people learned how to read and write. But the monks kept alive some Latin scholarship, at least from the later periods of the Roman Empire, as well as focusing on religious studies. The Dark Ages were not as gloomy and backward as some historians once thought, although they could seem that way compared to the greatness of Rome at its peak.

Missionaries–monks or other people who try to spread their faith to new regions–carried Greco-Roman culture beyond the borders of the old empire. Christianity reached Ireland for the first time, and it also extended into Ethiopia, in eastern Africa. In the east, the Byzantine Empire came into contact with a new cultural and political force: the Islamic Arab world. The Islamic religion grew out of the teachings of Muhammad (c. 570–632), with influences from both Judaism and Christianity. Through the Byzantine Empire, the Arabs learned about ancient Greek science and philosophy. Later, the Arabs helped Western European scholars rediscover classical writings and ideas that had been lost during the Dark Ages.

Starting in the 1300s, this reintroduction of Greco-Roman thought led to a burst of artistic and intellectual creativity in Western Europe. It reached its peak during the Renaissance–French for "rebirth." The Renaissance lasted through the first half of the 16th century. Artists returned to artistic styles and techniques common during Roman times and deliberately tried to copy the best works of Greco-Roman art. As the Renaissance progressed, artists also looked to Greek and Roman mythology for their subjects, turning away from Christian themes. Some artists also painted scenes from everyday life, just as Roman artists had done with

Mighty Jupiter
The Roman god is shown with a scepter in his left hand and a thunderbolt in his right. This is a third century C.E. Roman copy of a first century B.C.E. Greek statue. The classical Greek ideals of art, as passed on by the Romans, inspired the Renaissance.

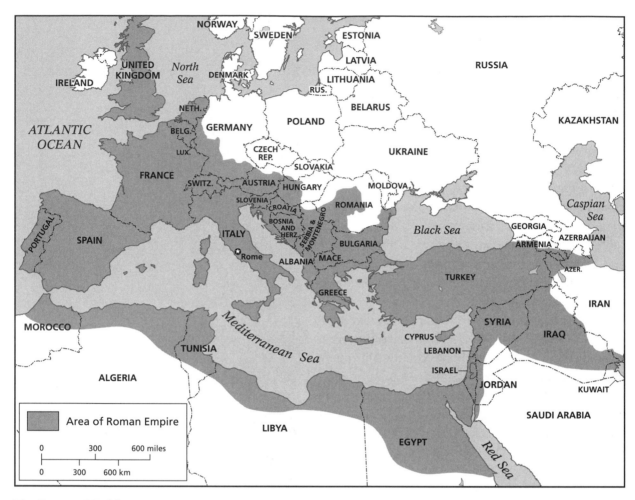

The Roman World

Roman influence shaped civilizations as far apart as Britain and Armenia.

their wall paintings and mosaics. Architects also looked to Roman influences, designing buildings with domes and columns similar to the ones used in Roman times.

The Renaissance affected writers as well. In Italy, the scholar Petrarch (1304–1374) helped create a philosophy known as humanism, which included the revival of classical learning and a devotion to the individual and critical spirit. He stressed the importance of studying the ancient Roman and Greeks, rather than merely reading the Bible and Christian philosophers. He read the Roman writers for the beauty of their words, and not just for the lessons they could teach. Italians also began to study ancient Greek and Latin. They wanted to read classic works in their original languages, not in translations using the modified Latin of their day. The rise of humanism eventually led to a new interest in science and philosophy separate from Church teachings. Well-educated Europeans saw themselves continuing a tradition dating from Greco-Roman times.

Through the 19th century, educated Americans and Europeans learned Latin—and sometimes Greek—so they could read the original words of classical writers. The political ideas of the Roman Republic shaped Americans as they tried to create their own government during the late 18th century. Many scholars might have agreed with Petrarch, who once wrote (as quoted by David Thompson in *The Idea of Rome*), "What is all history, other than the praise of Rome?"

The "Roman" World Today

Today, on three continents, dozens of modern nations exist within the borders of the old Roman Empire (see the box on page 45). These countries have different languages, religions, and political systems, but they share a tie to the ancient Roman world. And these countries, through conquest or immigration, helped spread Greco-Roman culture around the world.

As noted throughout this book, many modern geographic names come from Latin words or had their roots in the Roman era. One of the Celtic tribes that Julius Caesar battled was the Belgae; their name is the heart of the word Belgium. Romania's name came from the presence of Roman troops within its borders. And the Swiss sometimes call their country Helvetia, which came from the Latin name for another Celtic tribe defeated by the Romans. Many modern rivers also take their names from Latin. These include the Danube (Danuvius), Tiber (Tiberis), and Rhine (Rhenus). Modern names for seas that came from Roman names include the Mediterranean (Mediterraneum), Adriatic (Adriaticum), and Aegean (Aegeum).

The Modern Nations of the Roman Empire

Here are the nations that were once wholly or partly within the Roman Empire, or under direct Roman influence:

EUROPE	Hungary	Montenegro	Jordan
Andorra	Italy	Slovenia	Lebanon
Albania	Liechtenstein	Spain	Syria
Austria	Luxembourg	Switzerland	Turkey
Belgium	Macedonia	United	AFRICA
Bosnia and	Malta	Kingdom	Algeria
Herzegovina	Monaco	Vatican City	Egypt
Bulgaria	Netherlands	ASIA	Libya
Croatia	Portugal	Armenia	Morocco
France	Romania	Cyprus	Tunisia
Germany	San Marino	Iraq	
Greece	Serbia and	Israel	

117

The largest daily influence of Rome appears in the words people speak. Latin led to the development of a family of languages known as Romance languages. They include French, Italian, Spanish, Romanian, and Portuguese. Through conquest, several of these languages, particularly Spanish and French, are now spoken throughout the world. English has also been influenced by the Romance languages and by Latin itself, as

CONNECTIONS >>>>>>>>>>>>>>>

Rome to Monticello

Two popular tourist attractions in the United States trace their design to the Romans, through the influence of Renaissance architects. President Thomas Jefferson (1743–1826) modeled his home at Monticello, Virginia, after the work of the 16th-century Italian architect Andrea Palladio (1508–1580). Palladio had visited Rome to study the ancient buildings, which inspired his work. Monticello, which was designed by Jefferson, was the first home in the United States to have a Roman-style dome. The design of the Jefferson Memorial in Washington, D.C., built in 1939 in honor Jefferson, echoes the president's blueprints for his Monticello home. Compare it to the picture of the Pantheon on page 96.

The Jefferson Memorial in Washington, D.C., reflects the president's admiration for classical Roman aesthetics.

has been noted throughout this book. Latin is still taught in schools across the West, though not as extensively as in the past, and some Roman Catholic churches still use it during their services. Latin is also the official language of the Vatican, the seat of the Roman Catholic Church.

For several decades, but especially since the start of the 21st century, some scholars and journalists have argued that the United States is similar to a modern-day Roman Empire. Like Rome, the United States is the world's undisputed military power. And although the United States does not control many overseas territories, it has an economic and cultural influence that matches the "Romanization" process of imperial Rome. The United States also has a military presence in many countries, meaning its troops can quickly take action around the world, just as the emperors had legions stationed across the empire. The United States, like Rome, attracts people from many different ethnic and religious backgrounds, and these many groups play important roles in society.

CONNECTIONS >>>>>>>>>>>>

Latin Phrases Today

Latin not only shaped many English words; some complete Latin phrases are still commonly used in English. Here's a sample:

ad nauseum: to the point of nausea; something done to a sickening or excessive degree

casus belli: the cause of a war

de facto: in fact or in practice

e pluribis unum: from many, one (the motto of the United States)

non sequitur: it does not follow; used to describe an illogical statement

persona non grata: person not wanted; a person who has done something that angers others

quid pro quo: a thing for a thing; an exchange of favors

However, the United States does not have an emperor who serves for life. And most Americans do not think the country should be actively trying to control other lands, while the Romans believed they were destined to rule the world. Still, as journalist Charles Krauthammer told *The New York Times*, "The fact is, no country has been as dominant culturally, economically, technologically and militarily in the history of the world since the Roman Empire" (quoted by Jonathan Freedland in the British newspaper *The Guardian)*.

An empire or not, the United States, like the rest of the Western world, maintains traditions and cultural activities that the Romans developed more than 2,000 years ago.

TIME LINE

753 B.C.E. According to Roman legends, Romulus founds the city of Rome.

509 B.C.E. According to traditional sources, Romans kill their last king and create the Republic.

494 B.C.E. The plebeians form their own assembly and begin electing their own magistrates, called tribunes.

338 B.C.E. Rome wins the Latin War, ensuring its dominance in central Italy.

264 B.C.E. The First Punic War begins, and for the first time, Roman forces fight off the Italian mainland.

146 B.C.E. Rome defeats Carthage in the Third Punic War, confirming its dominance of the western Mediterranean.

133 B.C.E. Tiberius Gracchus is elected tribune, and he and his brother Gaius begin a reform program to help Rome's lower classes.

88 B.C.E. Marius and Sulla command opposing troops during Rome's first civil war.

46 B.C.E. The dictatorship of Julius Caesar begins, ending the Republic.

27 B.C.E. Octavian is given the title Augustus and rules what is now officially the Roman Empire.

C. 29 C.E. The Romans crucify a Jewish teacher named Jesus, leading to the development of Christianity.

64 A huge fire destroys half of Rome.

110s The emperor Trajan expands the borders of the empire to their largest extent.

235 The empire enters a period of political chaos that lasts 50 years.

286 Diocletian splits the empire into eastern and western halves and chooses a co-emperor to rule with him.

313 Constantine the Great allows Christians to freely practice their faith, ending almost three centuries of persecution.

324 Constantine reunites the two halves of the empire and later moves his capital from Rome to Byzantium, later renamed Constantinople.

395 The empire again splits into eastern and western halves, with the eastern half emerging as the more powerful of the two; it is later known as the Byzantine Empire.

476 The last Roman emperor in the west is replaced by a Germanic king.

RESOURCES: Books

Amery, Colin, and Brian Curran Jr. *The Lost World of Pompeii* (The J. Paul Getty Museum, 2002)

> When Mount Vesuvius erupted in 79, it covered the cities of Pompeii and Herculaneum, preserving everything from elegant villas to workers' homes, offering a complete picture of everyday life in a Roman town. This book provides more than 150 new photographs of the ruins and the artifacts found in them, and covers the history of the city, the discovery of the remains, the town plan, the private life of Pompeii, Pompeii's design legacy, and the site today.

Conti, Flavio. *A Profile of Ancient Rome* (The J. Paul Getty Museum, 2003)

> Written by an Italian scholar who specializes in Roman history and architecture, this book covers the entire history of Rome, with an especially detailed look at Roman building projects and monuments.

Cornell, Tim, and John Matthews. *Atlas of the Roman World* (Checkmark Books, 1982)

> More than just a collection of maps, this book has solid historical research on the history of Rome, along with features on such topics as festivals, art, technology, and the army.

Dersin, Denise, editor. *What Life Was Like When Rome Ruled the World: The Roman Empire, 100 B.C.–A.D. 200* (Time-Life Books, 1997)

> With many colorful illustrations and photos, this book vividly examines both political developments and daily activities as Rome moved from the Republic to the Empire and expanded its borders on three continents.

Hamilton, Edith. *Mythology: Timeless Tales of Gods and Heroes* (Warner Books, 1999)

> This recent edition of a classic book introduces all the important figures in Greek and Roman mythology, drawing on the original sources from ancient times.

Hazel, John. *Who's Who in the Roman World* (Routledge, 2001)

> Hazel presents biographical information on more than 1,000 Romans from all walks of life and includes family trees for some of the more prominent people featured. The book also includes a glossary and several maps.

Le Bohec, Yann. *The Imperial Roman Army* (Routledge, 2000)

> An in-depth look at the military force that helped build the Roman Empire, this book examines the training of the soldiers and the tactics they used in battle. It also looks at the impact the imperial army had on Roman society.

Nardo, Don. *Rulers of Ancient Rome* (Lucent Books, 1999)

> This book offers short biographies on some of the important rulers who shaped Rome's history, including Marius, the general who started the trend toward one-man rule; Augustus, the first emperor; and Justinian, the eastern emperor who tried to reunite the empire.

Shelton, Jo-Ann. *As the Romans Did* (Oxford University Press, 1998)

> This book collects the writings of ancient historians, politicians, poets, and others to give a first-hand look at life in Rome. Shelton also provides useful background information before the primary sources.

RESOURCES: Web Sites

Encyclopaedia Romana

itsa.ucsf.edu/~snlrc/encyclopaedia_romana/index.html

> This site offers essays on a wide range of subjects, including Roman architecture, some of the Roman provinces, and important people. A detailed index makes it easy to find references to almost any subject.

Roman Imperial Forums

www.capitolium.org/english.htm

> Sponsored by the city of Rome, this site provides information on archaeological research going on in Rome, as well as general information on the Empire. The web site also has photos of prominent Roman ruins, and two webcams provide live shots of Rome today.

Internet Ancient History Sourcebook: Rome

www.fordham.edu/halsall/ancient/asbook09.html#Literature

> Part of a huge online "library" of primary sources, the Roman sourcebook includes the writings of some of Rome's most famous historians and poets, as well as links to other sites with information on Roman history and primary sources for other empires that came before and after Rome.

Nova Roma—Via Romana

www.novaroma.org/via_romana/

> Nova Roma, or "New Rome," provides information on the Via Romana—"the Roman way." This section of the website has guidelines for choosing a Roman name, and a calculator that converts Roman numerals to Arabic and vice versa (a Latin phrase meaning "conversely" or "in the opposite order"). The Via Romana also has information on Roman reenactments.

Illustrated History of the Roman Empire

www.roman-empire.net

> An incredibly detailed site with such features as a timeline, interactive maps, a special section for children and teens, and an online quiz so users can test their knowledge of Roman history.

Rome: Republic to Empire

www.vroma.org/~bmcmanus/romanpages.html

> Created by a college professor, this site offers a detailed look at such topics as Spartacus and his slave rebellion, the Roman army, and gladiatorial games.

BIBLIOGRAPHY

Adkins, Lesley, and Adkins, Roy A., *Handbook to Life in Ancient Rome, Updated Edition*. New York: Facts On File, 2004.

Ammianus, "The Battle of Adrianople." *The Book of Deeds*, Hillsdale College. URL: http://www.hillsdale.edu/oldacademics/history/War/Classical/Rome/378-Adrianople.htm. (Excerpt from Charles D. Yonge, *The Roman History of Ammianus Marcellinus During the Reigns of the Emperors Constantius, Julian, Jovianus, Valentinian, and Valens*. London: 1862). Updated 2003.

Boardman, John, et al., eds., *The Oxford Illustrated History of the Roman World*. New York: Oxford University Press, 1988.

Cantor, Norman, ed., *The Encyclopedia of the Middle Ages*. New York: Viking, 1999.

Clayton, Edward, "Cicero." Internet Encyclopedia of Philosophy. URL: http://www.utm.edu/research/iep/c/cicero.htm. Published 2001.

Cornell, Tim, and Matthews, John, *Atlas of the Roman World*. New York: Checkmark Books, 1982.

Dersin, Denise, ed., *What Life Was Like When Rome Ruled the World: The Roman Empire, 100 B.C.–A.D. 200*. Alexandria, Va.: Time-Life Books, 1997.

Downie, David, *Cooking the Roman Way*. New York: Harper-Collins, 2002.

Einhard. "Life of Charlemagne, Extracts from Book III." Internet Medieval Sourcebook. URL:http://www.fordham.edu/halsall/source/einhard1.html. (Excerpt from *Einhard, Life of Charlemagne*, S. E. Turner, translator. New York: Harper and Brothers, 1880.) Posted February 1996.

Electronic Text Center, University of Virginia Library. "Livy's History of Rome: Book 22, The Disaster of Cannae." URL: http://wyllie.lib.virginia.edu:8086/perl/toccer-ew?id=Liv3His.sgm&images=images/modeng&data=/texts/english/modeng/parsed&tag=public&part=2&division=div1. Updated August 2003.

Freedland, Jonathan, "Rome AD...Rome DC?" *Guardian Online*. URL: http://www.guardian.co.uk/usa/story/0,12271,794163,00.html. Posted September 18, 2002.

Gardner, Helen, *Art Through the Ages*, Rev. ed. New York: Harcourt Brace Jovanovich, 1975.

Geanakoplos, Deno J., *Medieval Western Civilization and the Byzantine and Islamic World*. Lexington, Ky.: D.C. Heath and Company, 1979.

Grant, Michael, *The Antonines: The Roman Empire in Transition*. New York: Routledge, 1994.

—, *History of Rome*. New York: Charles Scribner's Sons, 1978.

Hooper, Finley, *Roman Realities*. Detroit, Mich.: Wayne State University Press, 1979.

Horace, "The Pleasures of Country Life," Latin-UK-Online. URL: http://www.latin-ukonline.com/heuix/5.3horacemartialovid.html. (Excerpt from *Cambridge Latin Anthology*, Cambridge, U.K.: Cambridge Univsersity Press.) Published in 2000.

Illustrated History of the Roman Empire. "Which modern day countries did the Roman Empire comprise?" URL: http://www.roman-empire.net/maps/empire/extent/rome-modern-day-nations.html. Updated June 2003.

James, Peter, and Thorpe, Nick, *Ancient Inventions*. New York: Ballantine Books, 1994.

Jordanes, "History of the Goths, Chapter 20." Internet Ancient History Sourcebook. URL: http://www.fordham.edu/halsall/ancient/jordanes-goths20.html. (Excerpt from William Stearns Davis, ed., *Readings in Ancient History: Illustrative Extracts from the Sources, Vol. II: Rome and the West*. Boston: Allyn and Bacon, 1912-13.) Published June 1998.

Kaplan, Justin, ed., *Bartlett's Familiar Quotations*, 16th edition. Boston: Little, Brown and Company, 1992.

Livy, *Rome and the Mediterranean*. Translated by Henry Bettenson. Baltimore: Penguin Books, 1976.

Macrone, Michael, *By Jove!: Brush Up Your Mythology*. New York: Cader Books, 1992.

Merriam Webster's Collegiate Dictionary. 10th ed. Springfield, Mass.: Merriam Webster, 1997.

Merriam Webster's Geographical Dictionary. 3rd ed. Springfield, Mass.: Merriam Webster, 1997.

Polybius, "The Character of Hannibal." Internet Ancient History Sourcebook. URL: http://www.fordham.edu/halsall/ancient/polybius-hannibal.html. (Excerpt from *Polybius, The Histories of Polybius*, Evelyn S. Shuckburgh, translator. London: Macmillan, 1889.) Posted July 1998.

Plutarch, *The Lives of the Noble Grecians and Romans*. Translated by John Dryden. Chicago: Encyclopedia Britannica, 1990.

Pritchard, James B., ed., *The Harper Concise Atlas of the Bible*. New York: HarperCollins, 1991.

Procopius, "Secret History, Chapter VII." Internet Medieval Sourcebook. URL: http://www.fordham.edu/halsall/source/procop-anec1.html. Published March 1996.

Shakespeare, William, "The Tragedy of Julius Caesar." *The Complete Works of William Shakespeare*. New York: Doubleday, 1936.

Shelton, Jo-Ann, *As the Romans Did: A Sourcebook in Roman Social History*, 2nd ed. New York: Oxford University Press, 1998.

Sherk, Robert, editor and translator. *Translated Documents of Greece and Rome. Volume 6: The Roman Empire, Augustus to Hadrian*. New York: Cambridge University Press, 1988.

Suetonius, *The Twelve Caesars*. Translated by Robert Graves. New York: Penguin Books, 1992.

Tacitus, *The Annals and the Histories*. Translated by Alfred John Church and William Jackson Brodribb. Chicago: Encyclopedia Britannica, 1990.

Thompson, David, ed., *The Idea of Rome: From Antiquity to the Renaissance*. Albuquerque, N.M.: University of New Mexico Press, 1971.

Virgil, *The Aeneid*. Translated by Rolfe Humphries. New York: Charles Scribner's Sons, 1951.

Ward, Allen; Heichelheim, Fritz M.; and Yeo, Cedric, *A History of the Roman People*. 4th ed. Upper Saddle River, N.J: Prentice Hall, 2003.

Wells, Colin, *The Roman Empire*. 2nd ed. Cambridge, Mass.: Harvard University Press, 1992.

INDEX

Page numbers followed by *i* indicate illustrations.